D1206327

PREACHING THE PARABLES

Series II, Cycle A

WILLIAM E. KEENEY

CSS Publishing Company, Inc.
Lima, Ohio

PREACHING THE PARABLES, A

Copyright © 1995 by
CSS Publishing Company, Inc.
Lima, Ohio

All rights reserved. No part of this publication may be reproduced in any manner whatsoever without prior permission of the publisher, except in the case of brief quotations embodied in critical articles and reviews. Inquiries should be addressed to: Permission, CSS Publishing Company, Inc., 517 South Main Street, P.O. Box 4503, Lima, Ohio 45802-4503.

Scripture quotations are from the *New Revised Standard Version of the Bible*, copyright 1989, by the Division of Christian Education of the National Council of the Churches of Christ in the USA. Used by permission.

Library of Congress Cataloging-in-Publication Data

Keeney, William E. (William Echard), 1922-
    Preaching the parables : Series II, Cycle A / William E. Keeney.
        p.   cm.
    ISBN 0-7880-0541-3
    1. Jesus Christ—Parables. 2. Bible. N.T. Gospels—Homiletical use. 3. Preaching.
I. Title.
BT375.2.K386   1995
251'.02—dc20   95-14048
                                                                                    CIP

This book is available in the following formats, listed by ISBN:
0-7880-0541-3 Book
0-7880-0542-1 IBM 3 1/2 computer disk
0-7880-0543-x IBM 3 1/2 book and disk package
0-7880-0544-8 Macintosh computer disk
0-7880-0545-6 Macintosh book and disk package
0-7880-0546-4 IBM 5 1/4 computer disk
0-7880-0547-2 IBM 5 1/4 book and disk package

PRINTED IN U.S.A.

Dedication

This volume is dedicated to all the great preachers whom I have heard and who by their proclamation of Christian truth have given inspiration and shown the powerful impact of the spoken word.

Editor's Note Regarding The Lectionary

During the past two decades there has been an attempt to move in the direction of a uniform lectionary among various Protestant denominations.

•Lectionary Uniformity

Preaching on the same scripture lessons every Sunday is a step in the right direction of uniting Christians of many faiths. If we are reading the same scriptures together we may also begin to accomplish other achievements. Our efforts will be strengthened through our unity.

•Christian Unity

Beginning with Advent 1995 The Evangelical Lutheran Church in America will drop its own lectionary schedule and adopt the Revised Common Lectionary.

•ELCA Adopts Revised Common Lectionary

We at CSS Publishing Company heartily embrace this change. We recognize, however, that there will be a transitional period during which some churches may continue for a time to use the traditional Lutheran lectionary. In order to accommodate these clergy and churches who may still be referring to the Lutheran lectionary we will for a period of time continue to provide sermons and illustrations based on scriptural passages from BOTH the Lutheran and The Revised Common lectionaries.

•For Those In Transition

Table Of Contents

Introduction

Parables are a rich means of conveying spiritual truth and addressing problems. Jesus used a very basic teaching principle with them. He began with the familiar and moved to the unfamiliar. He used ordinary events which the hearers would readily recognize to communicate spiritual truths.

The parables of Jesus tell a brief story. They are short enough to remember but long enough to stir the imagination and make a point. They use some experience that would be common to the people to whom they were addressed. The persons hearing the parables could no doubt put themselves in the situation.

Generally the parables had only a single theme or answered a single question. While the early church often treated them as allegories and sought to find some spiritual meaning in every detail, today most people who use the parables would not try to press such meaning upon the parables. Where the parables have some allegorical interpretation, a guide is given for interpretation. Thus they are not left to free flight of the imagination in understanding them.

The parables were set in a particular culture. As noted, the experiences would have been common to the people who heard them. We live in a somewhat different culture. Nevertheless, most people can readily grasp the main meaning from the story. At times, however, explanation of the customs and practices of first century Palestine will help people have a fuller understanding of some of the parables.

Background of Matthew

In Cycle A of the Lectionary we have 14 parables. Only the parable for Easter is not from Matthew. It is from John and reflects on the person and role of Jesus. The other parables in the series do not refer to Jesus but to the nature of the kingdom of heaven. He may be identified in some of the parables as one of the actors.

A central theme of Matthew is the proclamation of the kingdom of heaven. Matthew gives it as the central theme of the preaching for both John the Baptist (Matthew 3:1, 2) and Jesus (Matthew 4:17).

Other characteristics of Matthew are:

•Matthew emphasizes the royalty of Jesus. For example, in the birth narratives only Matthew has the report of the coming of the wise men to honor Jesus.

•Matthew is addressed to Hebrew Christians. He frequently refers to the Old Testament and assumes his readers are familiar with it. He is interested in fulfillment of the Old Testament passages.

•Matthew includes five major blocks of teaching materials which are inserted into a narrative which follow very closely the chronology of the Gospel according to Mark.

•Matthew apparently used sources other than Mark. He has some material which is common to Luke and not to Mark. He also has materials not found in any of the other Gospels and so must have come from some independent source which only he used.

Of the parables from Matthew in this series, all but two are found in Matthew only, though Luke has variations or echoes of two of them. Two are found in both Mark and Luke as well.

As Matthew moves through the account of Jesus' life, the parables tend to move from joy in finding the kingdom to judgment for rejection of it.

The Literary Form of the Parables

A parable is a particular type of story. It casts some familiar story along side of some spiritual truth. This makes the spiritual truth more understandable for the common people.

A parabolic curve is named for the same idea. It is a curve whose arms have a radius so that the two arms of the curve become parallel only at infinity. A parabolic curve is contrasted to a hyperbolic curve where the radius of the arms is such that they become perpendicular to each other at infinity.

Thus we see the elements of a parable as being similar, or running alongside each other. The elements of hyperbole move away from each other by means of exaggeration. An example of hyperbole would be Jesus' statement that it is easier for a camel to go through the eye of a needle than for a rich man to enter the kingdom of heaven. (Matthew 19:24, Mark 10:25, Luke 18:25).

Story telling is an ancient art. It is always used widely in cultures that depend primarily on oral communication. Story telling tickles the imagination. Jesus did not so much engage in rational abstraction to teach. He tried to make his teachings concrete. He was not irrational but moved beyond rationality to affect the heart of the hearers as well as the mind.

The use of parables was especially appropriate for Jesus' style of communication. As far as we know Jesus put nothing in writing to be preserved. Indeed, the Gospels were probably not put into written form for 30 to 40 years after the crucifixion. They were passed along orally. Only when those who had heard Jesus personally began to pass off the scene were they reduced to writing. Stories such as the parables would be easy to memorize and repeat. Thus they were preserved and incorporated into the Gospel accounts which we have.

Use of the Material

This book does not provide full sermons. Instead it gives helpful materials to stimulate your own sermon preparation.

Where appropriate, help is given in understanding the context of the reading in terms of the church year and the lectionary. Some help will be given in exegesis of the parables. As noted above, some explanation may be useful to understand the cultural context of the parables.

Major themes or issues which arise from the parables will be suggested. They can be used to develop various theological concepts.

The parables are not just interesting or curious stories. They were applied to questions or problems which Jesus faced in his time. They must be applied to the needs of the church in our time. Sermon suggestions and possible outlines will be proposed.

Every sermon needs illustrations. They provide windows of light into the sermon. Several possible illustrations will be given for each parable.

May the Spirit guide you as you reflect upon the parables and seek to communicate the message they should carry to your congregation today.

1. Seasoning And Illumination

Matthew 5:13-20

"You are the salt of the earth; but if salt has lost its taste, how can its saltiness be restored? It is no longer good for anything, but is thrown out and trampled under foot.

14"You are the light of the world. A city built on a hill cannot be hid. 15No one after lighting a lamp puts it under the bushel basket, but on the lampstand, and it gives light to all in the house. 16In the same way, let your light shine before others, so that they may see your good works and give glory to your Father in heaven.

17"Do not think that I have come to abolish the law or the prophets; I have come not to abolish but to fulfill. 18For truly I tell you, until heaven and earth pass away, not one letter, not one stroke of a letter, will pass from the law until all is accomplished. 19Therefore, whoever breaks one of the least of these commandments, and teaches others to do the same, will be called least in the kingdom of heaven, but whoever does them and teaches them will be called great in the kingdom of heaven. 20For I tell you, unless your righteousness exceeds that of the scribes and Pharisees, you will never enter the kingdom of heaven."

Salt is very important to life. If a person lacks salt, the hunger for it is one of the strongest desires we have. Any farmer knows how cattle will find a salt block and lick it to maintain the proper balance in its body. Salt is so valuable that in some societies it has been used as a medium of exchange, a substitute for money.

In the scripture, light is often used as a symbol for the existence of God. It is frequently used in a variety of ways throughout the Bible. In some cultures the sun was worshiped as a source of life and became a symbol for deity.

Salt and light are universal symbols and so these two brief statements in the Sermon on the Mount have a powerful effect.

While Jesus reinterprets the commandments of the Old Testament in the light of his higher understanding, he affirms them and asserts that they will not pass away.

Context

Context of the Church Year

The parable comes early in Jesus' ministry as part of the Sermon on the Mount. The Sunday for this reading is fairly early between Christmas as the celebration of Jesus' birth and Easter as the celebration of his resurrection.

Context of Matthew 5

The passage in Matthew 5:13-16 follows immediately after the Beatitudes as part of the Sermon on the Mount. The Beatitudes are not individual characteristics of Christians. They are a composite of those who are citizens of the kingdom of heaven. The composite is a good description of the person of Jesus himself. Jesus uses the symbols of salt and light to summarize the effect which persons who exhibit the characteristics of the beatitudes have in society.

Context of the Lectionary

The First Lesson. (Isaiah 58:1-9a) The text has as one part the proclamation, "Then your light shall break forth like the dawn" (Isaiah 58:8). Isaiah 58:10 also says, "Then your light shall rise in the darkness." Jesus has echoes of the passage in saying that those who enter the kingdom are the light of the world. In

Isaiah the light depends on doing justice, feeding the hungry and meeting the needs of the afflicted.

The Second Lesson. (1 Corinthians 2:1-12) Paul asserts that when he came to the Corinthians he sought to preach nothing but Christ crucified. That is the wisdom that comes from the mystery of God. It is revealed through the spirit of God to the human spirit. It is a gift given to those receptive to hear it.

Gospel. (Matthew 5:13-20) The reading from the gospel includes the beatitudes as well as the two brief similes or parables. The parables are the consequence of those who respond to the call of the presence of the kingdom of God and manifest the characteristics given in the beatitudes.

The Psalm. (Psalm 112:1-9) The theme of light is also found in this passage, "They rise in darkness as a light for the upright, they are gracious, merciful, and righteous." Mercy and righteousness are part of the Beatitudes and such characteristics become light in the believer.

Context of the Scriptures

In Genesis 1:1-3 separating light from darkness is the first activity of God in creation. Jesus in John 8:12 makes the claim, "I am the light of the world." In Isaiah 42:6 Israel is given the challenge, "I have given you as a covenant to the people, a light to the nations." In Luke 2:30-32, Simeon sees Jesus as the fulfillment of this demand, "For my eyes have seen your salvation, which you have prepared in the presence of all peoples, a light for revelation to the Gentiles, and for the glory to your people Israel."

> Job 6:6 — Job asks the question, "Can that which is tasteless be eaten without salt?
> Psalm 119:105 — The word is described as a lamp to guide.
> Jeremiah 25:10 — The lamp will be banished.
> Mark 9:49-50 — A somewhat parallel passage to Matthew about the salt losing its saltiness.

John 1:4-5 — Life and light related with light overcoming darkness.

John 8:12 — "I am the light of the world."

Ephesians 5:8-9 — Ephesians admonished to be children of light.

1 Thessalonians 5:5 — Thessalonians called children of light.

2 Peter 1:19 — The Christians to be as a lamp shining in a dark place.

Context of the Pericope

Both the images of salt and light are not simply consequences for the believers as citizens of the kingdom of heaven. They are the function the citizens have in a world living outside of obedience to God, in darkness. They are the ways in which citizens of the kingdom serve to redeem the world.

Thesis. Citizens of the kingdom of heaven are to be representatives of that kingdom to the world as salt and light.

Theme. Give glory to God by witnessing to the society around us about the kingdom of heaven.

Key Words in the Parable

1. "Salt." (v. 13) Two major functions salt has for the hearers of the parable can be noted. The first was as a flavor. It is one of the four primary tastes. The others are sweet, sour, and bitter. Thus it was a seasoning. The second was as a preservative. In an age which did not have refrigeration it was especially important in keeping food from spoiling.

2. "Earth." (v. 13) It is not to be taken as the physical world, but the entire inhabited world.

3. "Lost its taste." (v. 13) It has to be understood in

terms of salt that was not pure sodium chloride. Other impurities were mixed with the salt commonly used. At times the real salt would be so diluted in the mixture that what was left no longer seasoned food. It had the appearance of salt but had lost its saltiness.

4. "Thrown out." (v. 13) That which no longer had enough salt to season or preserve food was discarded. It no longer had the value it was intended to serve.

5. "Trampled under foot." (v. 13) What did you do with the residue that is no longer useful? You had to exercise care in disposing it. It might still have enough chemical reaction to spoil the land used for growing food. It was frequently thrown onto a road or path where it would do no harm and would provide a smooth surface to walk upon.

6. "Light." (vv. 14-15) Light is an elemental need. Without it life would be impossible. All life on earth depends either directly or indirectly on light. The biologists tell us that even the organisms which live so deeply in the ocean that no sunlight penetrates still depend for nourishment on chemical substances that settle down from above. These materials were formed by reactions with light. The ability to store energy from light through photosynthesis is characteristic of all plants and is basic to all living matter on earth. Light was often used in the Bible as contrasted to darkness and as life as opposed to death.

7. "A city built on a hill." (v. 14) This reference suggests the communal nature of the kingdom. It is not "points of light" that matter, but the accumulative nature of the light that is visible to the world and cannot be hid. Christianity is not just a private and inward experience. It is by its nature visible and public in a community with others. The hearers at the time would probably have thought immediately of Jerusalem, the sacred city, in all its splendor.

8. "Lamp." (v. 15) A lamp was the main source of light other than daylight in a Jewish household. It dispelled the darkness and provided illumination. We may be so accustomed to living with lighted streets and houses that it may be hard to realize how central a small lamp might be.

9. "Lampstand." (v. 15) A typical lamp in Jesus' time would be a clay container filled with oil and a wick in it. It would not cast a great amount of light. People placed it on a lampstand so that it would light the whole room, usually only one room for the household. They had to conserve resources so a lamp had to provide maximum usefulness.

10. "Good works." (v. 16) Citizens of the kingdom of heaven are presumed to do good works. They are evidence of the character of the kingdom's members. Good works should be self-evident signs of kingdom citizenship. The beatitudes are not just nice ideals; they should become operational in good works.

11. "Glory." (v. 16) The good works are not an occasion of pride or self-glorification. They reflect to the glory of the head of the kingdom who is the source of the light.

Contemplation

1. Diverse colors. Light has a diversity to it. In its fullness it is seen as white. In a variety of ways it may be broken into its component parts, filtered, or absorbed in part. That gives the wide array of color that we enjoy. In the same way, members of the Christian community in their diversity may offer a variety of color. It is when they are merged into the church that they shine forth in full brilliance of white light.

2. Christians shine. Christians may shine forth in the world in many ways. They may be called to serve the needs of the hungry. They may find that they must bring the good news of the kingdom in opposing injustice or in meeting the needs of the afflicted or the oppressed. They may be called to shed light into lives darkened by enslaving habits of various addictions. They may bear the burdens of those who live in fear, in sickness, in the threat of death.

3. The church in the world. The church may set up institutions and organizations which meet needs and offer alternatives to the usual ways of the world. Churches have been salt and light in establishing hospitals, schools, orphanages, homes for the aged, and other such service institutions. The saltiness often leads the world to adopt and extend these institutions once they are enlightened by the models which the church has provided.

4. Contemporary light and salt. Do the church and its members need to ask in every age how it can be light and salt? How do they provide models of God's intention for the way people ought to live in community and in society? By responding to needs with the guidance of the Holy Spirit the church continues to be salt and light today. With the breakdown of the family, the church needs to demonstrate what a family should be. By its care and support for each other it can illuminate what the family should provide. Where families have broken down, the church can help support those persons who do not find the light in the home.

Homily Hints

1. Salt of the World. (v. 13)
A. Salt as Seasoning. How do members of the kingdom of heaven add taste to the life of the larger society in which they live?
B. Salt as Preservative. The world would fall into total chaos and life would be impossible if people live only for themselves. A society is preserved by those who are willing to serve the interests of the society.
C. From whence Saltiness? People need to have the impurities of life removed to have the full measure of saltiness. It is by submitting life to the cleansing by the

sovereign head of the kingdom that full saltiness is possible.

2. Light. (vv.14-16) Light has many functions and characteristics. People need to combine all of them for the fullness of light.

 A. Light as warmth and radiance.
 B. Light as illumination. It overcomes the darkness around us.
 C. Light as color. It is beautiful and lends pleasure to life.

3. Light of the World. (vv. 14-16) We receive the light from a source beyond ourselves, just as the world depends on the light of the sun.

 A. The Source of Energy. It is beyond ourselves in Jesus Christ as the light of the world. Just as sunlight provides the source of all our food for the physical body, the light of Christ feeds our spiritual body.
 B. Reflected Glory. We are more like the moon than the sun in that its light is only a reflection of the sun. Our light is a reflection of the light we receive from God.
 C. Overcoming Darkness. Light dispels the darkness of ignorance, selfishness, and other evils in the world.

4. What Kind of Light. (vv. 14-16) Light shines in different ways. Christians may also have different callings in letting their lights shine.

 A. Spotlights. They focus on narrow issues and concentrate the light.
 B. Floodlights. They diffuse their light and spread it over a broad area of illumination.
 C. Searchlights. They give direction to safe havens as lighthouses or searchlights at airports do.

5. A City on a Hill. (v. 14) The image is of a society. The church is the collective of the individual lights that compose it. Together they shine in a way that individual lights do not.

A. The Darkness of the World
B. The Light of the Church
C. The Light Shining in the World

Contact

Points of Contact

1. No one wants to be discarded. How often people complain that no one pays any attention to them. Or they complain that a spouse never listens to them. People want to be valued. They sometimes express the way they are used as being like a doormat. People walk over them and leave their dirt on them. The question arises as to whether such people have not demonstrated their worth. They do not have self-esteem and do not assert their own value. They are like salt that has lost its tastiness. They need to return to the source of saltiness. They need to realize their worth as children of God and manifest the saltiness that comes as they are empowered by the Holy Spirit to show forth their value to themselves, to others and to God.

2. Light usually indicates the presence of God in the scriptures. People need guidance and understanding to make sense of life. Children are afraid in the dark. They want a light left on to chase away the monsters of their imagination. God's light illuminates the darkness of the world. It makes sense of the chaos around us. Without light people stumble and bump into objects. In a real way, without the light of God people stumble and fall in a world of darkness. They need the light to find their way to life and to avoid the death of the soul. Light makes visible God's will so that they may know and follow it.

3. A lamp was put on a lampstand in a Palestinian home. It was raised up so that it could better illuminate a room. People who have a false sense of modesty hide their light under a bushel. They do not let people know what abilities they have for fear they will have to accept more responsibilities. They may also be afraid

to let people know that they are Christians. They risk giving offense or being given a hard time by those who are not Christian. Thereby they let their light be hidden. People need to be encouraged to put their lamps on a lampstand and let the light shine to the glory of God.

Points to Ponder

1. Salt when supplied in excess is not a good seasoning. If you put too much salt in food, it is no longer tasty. Try eating a tablespoon of salt alone. Or if you put salt in a fertile field, it is no longer fertile. The allies broke the dikes and let in the sea on the Island of Walchern in the Netherlands when they invaded the mainland of Europe in World War II. After the war the Dutch repaired the dikes and pumped out the salty water from the sea. It took several years of flushing the land with fresh water before it could be cultivated again.

When do Christians by use of wrong methods and self-righteous attitudes no longer serve as the salt of the earth? When do they become obnoxious and repulsive? Do they lose their saltiness when they impose standards of behavior on people by force because the people do not have the motivation and empowerment of the Holy Spirit to do what is demanded?

2. When does the light no longer illuminate? The story is told of a certain teacher who used brilliance not to enlighten but to dazzle. When you drive at night, you are advised not to look into the headlights of oncoming cars. If you do you will be blinded. You should look at the right side of the road and watch the oncoming car with peripheral vision.

It is a temptation when we use truth without love to dazzle people with the display of our light. Our truth should be tempered with love so as to enlighten those coming out of darkness.

Illustrative Materials

1. Living in Darkness. Not often do we experience total

darkness. In the depth of the Mammoth Cave in Kentucky you can experience total darkness. Fish who live in the waters in total darkness never develop eyes, so they have no sight. Persons who live in moral darkness do not develop sight and insight.

2. Sight while Blind. Helen Keller once was traveling through Connecticut. She commented that someone was using yellow paint. At first those traveling with her did not believe that, since she was blind, she could know that someone was painting with yellow paint. Then suddenly they realized that the strip in the center of the highway had recently been painted. She could "see" while blind!

3. Excess saltiness. Several fellows were living together while working on a job. They had made an agreement among themselves that they would take turns cooking. Anyone who complained about the food would next be the cook. The fellow who first started got tired of cooking and no one was making any complaints. He decided to force a complaint. In cooking rice he added a whole cup of salt to make it too salty. As they ate, one of the fellows could no longer keep silent. Finally he said, "This rice is sure salty," and then after a moment's hesitation added, "but that's the way I like it!"

4. Light in the Dark. Some fellows were at a camp in the mountains. One Sunday when they had free time four of them decided to go hiking. They took longer than expected and got off the trail as it turned dark. They got to the crest of a mountain and could see the light of the camp off in the distance, still two or three miles away. They decided to stay for the night since they could not see their way ahead and were not on a trail. In the morning they awoke and moved toward the camp. Just a short distance ahead of them in line with the camp, they suddenly saw a cliff over which they would probably have stumbled if they had continued without daylight to show the way.

5. Salt of the Earth. When the Roman Empire was

collapsing under the assault from the migrating tribes sweeping down from eastern Europe, some blamed the Christians for their troubles. They claimed that the Christians had offended the gods of Rome. Augustine of Hippo contended instead, and in fact it was, that the church preserved civilization and eventually brought the invading tribes into it.

6. Artificial Light. In Tucson, Arizona, the city has regulations against light pollution. The street lights are covered so that the light does not go into the sky. It is quite a contrast with Phoenix with all its garish neon signs along business areas. Tucson has regulations against light pollution because a major telescope is located on a nearby mountain. If all the artificial light of the city brightened the sky, it would obscure the natural lights from the stars. Do the artificial lights of the cities of the world obscure the brightness and glory of the natural light proceeding from God through Christ?

2. The Shepherd And His Flock

John 10:1-10

"Very truly, I tell you, anyone who does not enter the sheepfold by the gate but climbs in by another way is a thief and a bandit. ²The one who enters by the gate is the shepherd of the sheep. ³The gatekeeper opens the gate for him, and the sheep hear his voice. He calls his own sheep by name and leads them out. ⁴When he has brought out all his own, he goes ahead of them, and the sheep follow him because they know his voice. ⁵They will not follow a stranger, but they will run from him because they do not know the voice of strangers." ⁶Jesus used this figure of speech with them, but they did not understand what he was saying to them.

⁷So again Jesus said to them, "Very truly, I tell you, I am the gate for the sheep. ⁸All who came before me are thieves and bandits; but the sheep did not listen to them. ⁹I am the gate. Whoever enters by me will be saved, and will come in and go out and find pasture. ¹⁰The thief comes only to steal and kill and destroy. I came that they may have life, and have it abundantly."

Not many people today are very familiar with shepherding as it was done in the first century. They are familiar with the frequent use of the image of sheep and the shepherd if they have a background in the scriptures. Many pictures portray Jesus as a shepherd. It is embodied often in stain glass windows or in children's Sunday school materials.

Still, it is difficult to conceive of any other image today which would as satisfactorily communicate the caring and sacrificial nature of Jesus' ministry. What would convey the ideas as fully in the largely urbanized and industrialized culture of western civilization as a whole? Perhaps it would be the care that some people give their pets, though that would lack the sense of a flock that needs the care of a shepherd.

Perhaps it would be the doctor who looks after the health of a community. Even that lacks something of the personal attention and care, especially with our high-tech medical system and the tendency for detached specialization. Often the doctor is seen only briefly and other personnel are the primary contact for the patient.

So we need to continue to revert to the customs and practices of the shepherd and the meaning of sheep in the Near Eastern culture of Jesus' time. We need to fill it with the kind of meaning it would have had for Jesus' early companions and others who would have heard his teachings.

Context

Context of the Church Year

This reading of the Lectionary comes in the Easter season. It is the time when the church is most conscious of the sacrificial meaning of Jesus' death and resurrection. His care for his disciples and for his mother even in the midst of his suffering and agony in confronting the cross reinforce the image of him as a shepherd concerned for his flock.

Context of the Scripture

The scripture has many references to the shepherd and the sheep. In the Old Testament period, both for Israel and for countries around them, the king was considered a shepherd. You find the transfer of this to God in the Old Testament in passages such as Psalms 78:70-72, 118:20. The shepherd comes to be identified with God in Psalm 23 and 80, and Isaiah 40. The intruder into the flock or the sheepfold is alluded to in Jeremiah 23:1-4. Jesus certainly must have had Ezekiel 34 in mind when delivering John 10. In that passage a clear identification of the shepherd with a messiah king of David's type is given. While Jesus reinterprets the kind of messiah he is, somewhat different from the David type, the hearers familiar with Ezekiel 34 would most likely have made the connection between Jesus as the shepherd and the expectation of the shepherd messiah.

In Israel and later in Judaism, the sheep was the sacrificial animal acceptable to God. Jesus himself replaces it and thus the need for the use of a sheep as a substitute for human or animal sacrifice no longer is needed. The sacrifice of Jesus and the identification of his followers with his death and resurrection creates a new religious relationship for them. This is expressed in Hebrews 13:20 which describes Jesus as "the great shepherd of the sheep, by the blood of the eternal covenant."

Context of John 9 and 10

Some would contend that the events of John 9 finally convinced Jesus that he could not expect to reform the system of Judaism as an institution. The decision of the leaders to excommunicate from the synagogue any who would follow him led Jesus to conclude that some institutional form was needed to gather his followers together in community. They would consider the images of the sheep and the shepherd in chapter 10 the beginning of the church. The events in Acts where the church formally gathered and eventually became separate from Judaism have their origins here in the life of Jesus.

Context of the Lectionary.

The First Lesson. (Acts 2:42-47) This reading gives us the picture of the early church as it still gathered and attempted to stay within Judaism. While it continued in temple worship, it instituted other forms of communal worship and sharing to bring together and maintain the flock which followed Jesus as the shepherd.

The Second Lesson. (1 Peter 2:19-25) This passage is rich in the symbolism of the shepherd and the sheep. The example of Jesus who gave his life to save his sheep is the basic thought at the beginning of the lesson. It moves on to the continuing purpose of Jesus as the shepherd who saves the souls of those who follow him. Without following the shepherd, they are like sheep who go astray and fall victims to the dangers of the world.

Gospel. (John 10:1-10) The reading contains the familiar parable of the good shepherd. It portrays the type of ministry that Jesus exercises in gathering his followers after the decision in John 9 to expel from the synagogue those who confessed him as the Messiah.

Psalm 23. Persons who are ill, who face death, who are aware of the frailty of human life on this earth probably look to this psalm more frequently than any other. Pastors are asked to read this for persons seeking solace and comfort in such situations. For Christians, the image of Jesus as the shepherd would help them to personalize the care and support of God.

Putting it all Together

The sheep is a very vulnerable animal. It has no weapons to defend itself. It is also not a very bright animal. If it is separated from the flock and on its own, it can get lost. In the hilly country of Palestine, it could easily get into a situation where it would be stuck. It could fall over a precipice or its wool might get caught in brambles and it would not be able to extricate itself. In either case the sheep on its own would eventually die.

Jesus sees his followers as persons in need of help in order to be saved. In the midst of a world with all its allures and dangers, they need protection and aid. He offers that as the Good Shepherd and as the sacrificial lamb willing to bring them into the care and protection of God.

He also warns them against those who would exploit the human need for religious support and certainty. Such persons are the ones against whom he pronounced his harshest words. Because religion provides the transcendent meaning to human life, those who lead persons astray are the most dangerous. The blindness of the religious leaders who could not accept the healing of the blind man and his further response to Jesus is a model for all persons who may be rejected by those who are false religious leaders.

Content

Content of the Pericope

The pericope has two sections to it. The first is found in John 10:1-6 and the second in John 10:6-10.

In the first part the emphasis is on the persons who would prey on the sheep, who lack qualifications as the true shepherd. They are contrasted with the true shepherd who puts his very life at stake for the good of the sheep. The disciples do not yet understand the full import of the statement prior to the crucifixion and resurrection. They do not see the contrast between Jesus as the good shepherd and the religious leaders who had just prosecuted and rejected the man who would follow Jesus and find salvation in him.

The second part makes much more explicit Jesus' claim to be the messianic shepherd. The passage contains one of the "I am" claims of Jesus so frequently found in John and only in the gospel according to John. Jesus states, "I am the gate for the sheep." This reinforces another of his claims, "I am the way, the truth and the life." Jesus is the way people can enter into the kingdom and know salvation, the consequence is the discovery of the real meaning of life. Jesus' way is the way of life as contrasted with the way of death.

Key Words in the Parable

1. "Very Truly." (v. 1) For Jesus, truth is not propositional. It is real being; it is life. He emphasizes the point he is about to make by claiming that it reveals what is the reality, not the appearance of real existence.

2. "Sheepfold." (v. 1) The image here is of the typical enclosure for the sheep in Palestine. It was a courtyard surrounded by a stone wall. It was the entry way to the house as well as for the animals. It would provide a secure place for the sheep, protecting them from weather, predatory animals and thieves.

3. "Thieves/Bandits." (vv. 1, 8) A person's chief wealth often would consist of his sheep. They provided wool for clothing, milk to drink, meat for food, and even covering for a tent as shelter. Sheep also sometimes served as a medium for exchange. They also would provide the sacrificial animal for religious observances, both in the temple and in the passover meal in the home. They might serve as a burnt offering, a guilt offering or a peace offering. Thieves or bandits would seek to steal the animals for their own use. They might climb over the stone wall and take the animals if no one was standing guard over them.

4. "Gate." (vv. 2, 7) An opening in the stone wall allowed both persons and the animals to enter and leave in the normal way. Often no obstruction prevented either the animals or persons from entering and leaving freely. A shepherd would sleep across the entrance so that no bandits or wolves would enter easily or the sheep wander out from the security of the sheepfold.

5. "Hear his voice." (v. 3) Often a shepherd would be responsible for many sheep. Shepherds would be hired by owners to care for a few animals when someone did not have enough to make it worth spending full time caring for them. In a mixed flock it would be hard to separate the sheep belonging to different owners. An owner would be able to call his sheep and they would come to him. As sheep, we are to recognize the call that comes to us from a leader who is the authentic shepherd, the one to whom we should belong.

6. "Calls his own." (v. 3) The man born blind had recognized the validity of Jesus' claim. Just as sheep respond to the call of the one to whom they belong, those who belong to Jesus will recognize his voice and respond to him.

Homily Hints

1. What's in a Name. The name of Jesus is not just some magical mantra or term. It refers to his real character, both in his humanity and in his divinity. What then do we see in Jesus when we call upon his name?

A. Jesus shows the true meaning of humanity.

B. Jesus is the role model.

C. Following Jesus fulfills our humanity.

2. Life Abundant. A life centered in self is not a big enough meaning for life. Persons need to give themselves to something bigger, more meaningful, and with a larger purpose.

A. Losing life is finding it.

B. Self-preservation versus self-sacrificing.

C. True happiness is not the end, but the by-product.

3. Pastoral Leadership. In the church, the definition of leadership is different from the world. In the world it is self-assertion and self-seeking. In the church it is by servanthood, following the model of Jesus.

A. A Pastor leads by attraction, not force.

B. A Pastor leads by gaining trust of his followers.

C. A Pastor leads the flock by self-giving.

4. The Church as a Sheepfold. People need the care and support of community. The church can serve for those who are wounded in spirit and need time for support and protection.

A. Enter by Christ's call.

B. Find real community.

C. Welcomed and belong because of need.

D. Mutual support offered and received.

5. Know His Voice. (v. 4) False prophets appear from time to time. They claim to have a message from God and may attract a following. Persons need help in recognizing the false prophets from the genuine call of Jesus as the good Shepherd.

  A. Voice accords with scripture
  B. Voice does not serve self-interest
  C. Voice and life authentically relates to Christ

Points of Contact

1. Listen to Him. Jesus did not so much call people to believe him, but to follow him. Of course, one cannot follow a person very long unless one believes in him. In another sense, one cannot really test the reality of a person unless you follow closely enough to test whether his life and message is genuine. The final proof of a person's convictions about Jesus is the readiness to accept discipleship, to learn from him and to follow him so that the person's life shows that the character and nature of Christ has become a part of self. Just as sheep follow the good shepherd in implicit trust, the life of discipleship calls for following Jesus' teachings and commands in complete trust that it is conforming to the meaning of life.

2. Salvation by Jesus Alone. Salvation comes by a change of life. It is not enough to give some intellectual consent or to use some magic formula which guarantees salvation. Salvation comes by presenting oneself to the God whom Jesus revealed in his life and by accepting his saving grace. One then proceeds to show in life that the presence of his Holy Spirit has entered into one's life and renewed it, enabling one to live in obedience. Salvation is not simply a claim but becomes a reality. Life becomes like Jesus. Even those who may not have heard the story of Jesus but whose life manifests their response to the light of God given to them have understood something about Jesus without having the name to give to it. In this sense, salvation may be possible by grace because they have understood the reality which gives the full meaning to life as God intends it to be.

3. The Shepherd as a Model for Leadership. Jesus in the parable of the good shepherd gives another indication of the model for leadership in the kingdom and therefore in the church. It is not a leadership characterized by domination for the leader's privilege and power. Rather leadership is intended as servanthood. The good shepherd serves the interest of the sheep. Leadership in the church should not be a struggle for power and privilege for fulfillment of personal ambitions. It should be as an opportunity to serve the flock of God and manifest God's love even to those in the world not part of God's flock.

4. The Church under Persecution. In many parts of the world the church is in danger. In some countries with a large Moslem population, such as Egypt, Christians may be the target of terrorist attacks. It is often the leaders of the church who are particularly vulnerable. When Ethiopia was under a Marxist government, the Christian churches were suppressed. Their buildings were confiscated. Leaders were imprisoned. But the members met in homes and the church grew despite the persecution. A good shepherd will recognize the risk and will seek to provide for the flock; so in situations such as Ethiopia, the leaders continued to serve the congregations despite the dangers. Some Ethiopian churches grew despite the oppression and danger. When the Marxist rule collapsed with the end of the cold war, the churches proved to be larger than before and grew rapidly.

In Indonesia during the '60s, a group of Marxists tried to take over the government by revolution. They were opposed by a Moslem dominated government. A bloodbath resulted. Some Christian leaders were martyred because they did not identify with either party in the conflict and were then suspect by both. After the revolution was suppressed, many persons were attracted to the Christian church because of its stance during the war and its readiness to serve the needs of the people regardless of religious persuasion or political affiliation.

In China during the so-called Cultural Revolution, Christian leaders were arrested or forced into hard labor. They remained steadfast, nevertheless. When the Cultural Revolution was past and more toleration of diversity was permitted, the church emerged again and some of the leaders led a revival in the churches. Recently contacts which had remained essentially ruptured since World War II were renewed and a faithful remnant was discovered to be present yet. A church independent of a mission or missionaries survived under local leadership.

5. Gang Membership. People get their identity in part from community. A problem with our urban and mass society is the loss of community. Young people seeking identity form gangs to recover a sense of identity and a support community. Usually the gangs have been males. More recently accounts are told of young women who want to be members of the gang. A roll of the dice tells how many members of the gang they must sleep with to be initiated into the gang.

Gang membership is not a true community. It does not point the way to life. It often leads to death, either from contracting AIDS from the sexual relationships or in the gang warfare over turf, with the almost random drive-by shootings.

Some young people in the church have found their identity by the challenge of voluntary service. They have participated in such projects as Habitat for Humanity or helping in flood relief following the floods in the midwest in 1993, or in cleaning up after earthquakes in California. Young people who have challenges such as these do not need gangs to give them a sense of identity. They find a true community in the church and in reaching out in service.

True shepherds will provide leadership where persons can find a real sense of identity, a challenge to service, and a community of support that reaches beyond their own interests and needs.

6. Who is in the Sheepfold? While the sheepfold is a shelter for security for the sheep, it is in danger of becoming a barrier to others to enter. How does the church provide a place of shelter and security for its members without engendering an "us" versus "them" mentality? A good shepherd will be constantly alert to bring any who are willing into the sheepfold.

1. Respond to the Voice. An ambassador from a South American country was visiting a church-related college. On the way from the airport, he began to inquire of his host what the nature of the church was that supported the college. He asked about the beliefs of the college community. He became intrigued by what he was told. He asked for some literature about the college and its denomination. The host gave him a book about the history and beliefs of the college's supporting denomination.

The next morning the ambassador was very excited. He had found the book so interesting that he had stayed up all night reading it. His reaction to it was that it said what he had always believed but he had never had terms to express it fully. This book gave him the name for what he really believed.

2. In His Steps. A pastor in Kansas needed stories to tell a youth group to have them understand what Christianity is about. In each session, he told them a story to take them through a process of understanding. A reporter from a Chicago newspaper heard about the success he was having and the enthusiasm of the young people in response. He obtained permission to publish these stories as a serial in the newspaper. Eventually they were gathered into a book titled *In His Steps*. It became the most popular best-seller of its time, only exceeded by the Bible itself.

3. Leadership. Two five-year-old boys were playing together. They decided they were going to play parade. They got into a big argument about who was going to head the parade. The argument went on for some time. Finally, one of the boys said in exasperation, "Okay, you be the leader. Get behind me and let's go!" And the other boy did!

4. Power of the Name. Certain primitive people understood that the name of the person told something of the person's real nature. Thus you had in biblical times changes of names when persons changed character. Abram became Abraham; Jacob became Israel; Simon became Peter; and Saul became Paul. If you knew the name of the persons, you could have some power over them. Some people were reluctant to give persons their names for fear they would exercise some power over them and it might not be good.

In modern times people sometimes change their names because they want to project a different image of themselves than they had before. This frequently happens when persons go from grade school to high school, or high school to college. One way to do it is to switch to using the middle name from the first name. Others want to abandon a nickname which identified them with some characteristic which they hope they have outgrown or moved beyond.

3. Self-deception, Hearers And Doers

Matthew 7:21-29

"Not every one who says to me, 'Lord, Lord,' will enter the kingdom of heaven, but only the one who does the will of my Father in heaven. [22]On that day many will say to me, 'Lord, Lord, did we not prophesy in your name, and cast out demons in your name, and do many deeds of power in your name?' [23]Then I will declare to them, 'I never knew you; go away from me, you evildoers.'

[24]Everyone then who hears these words of mine and acts on them will be like a wise man who built his house on the rock. [25]The rain fell, the floods came, and the winds blew and beat on that house, but it did not fall, because it had been founded on rock. [26]And everyone who hears these words of mine and does not act on them will be like a foolish man who built his house on sand. [27]The rain fell, and the floods came, and the winds blew and beat against that house, and it fell—and great was its fall!"

[28]Now when Jesus had finished saying these things, the crowds were astounded at his teaching, [29]for he taught them as one having authority, and not as their scribes.

In the first part of 1994 heavy rains in California sent mud slides down the hills near Los Angeles. Houses were ruined by the slides. Heavy rains falling on areas that were denuded by earlier forest fires caused the slides. The persons who were affected by the mud slides looked to the government to help them rebuild their

37

houses. Should these people rebuild in the same locations? If they do, should those who have suffered by the mud slides get government help to rebuild in the same locations? Are they wise to continue rebuilding there?

The same question could be raised about the persons who build in the flood plain of the Mississippi River. The federal government declared the places where the river flooded a disaster area, making those who were victims eligible for aid.

English, a town in southern Indiana, had the downtown area flooded on a number of occasions because of the confluence of several streams. They decided after a recent flood to relocate the town on higher ground. With federal aid many of the businesses have already relocated. At this writing some of the private residences are being built on the hill east of town. A whole new community is being created.

Perhaps the question could be raised: Who are the wise and who the foolish persons or communities?

Context

Context of the Church Year

This parable occurs at the beginning of the Pentecost season of the church year. It is a time when preachers have the option of choosing a variety of approaches for their sermons and for the main emphasis of the worship service.

Choices include using some of the alternative readings for the sermon. Other alternatives would be to set up a series which would be based on some theme or related topics of the preacher's choice.

Context of the Sermon on the Mount

The parable comes at the conclusion of the Sermon on the Mount and is a summary of the admonitions given in the sermon. It calls on those who heard the Sermon to take the admonitions seriously. They are not just to be enjoyed as a mind game, but to be translated in life. The persons who understand that what the Sermon on the Mount is calling them to do is the proper foundation for life must also realize the admonitions have to become operational, not merely accepted as general principles to be believed.

Context of the Gospel Lesson

The parable is a short one, taking up only four verses in the gospel lesson for today. It leads to the conclusion which Matthew draws in reporting the astonishment of the crowd who heard it. His teaching is contrasted with that of the scribes who were legalistic and often pedantic. Jesus demonstrated a vitality and dynamic that came out of his own life and experience. The integrity of his own life contributed to the validity of his message.

Context of the Parallel Parable

Both Matthew and Luke have the parable as the concluding section of a chapter. Luke has some slight differences, probably arising from his background outside of Palestine. Whereas Matthew has the house built on rock or sand, Luke says that the person who built on the rock dug down through the sand. Luke also suggests that both houses were well-built, but that the man who built on the rock had to dig down through the sand to find the rock.

Matthew probably had the awareness of someone in Palestine who might build in a dry *wadi*, a stream bed that would be dry during most of the year. In Palestine practically all rain comes between October and April. Rain is scarce and sparse between April and October. A person who builds in a wadi during the dry season might have the residue of the sand beneath the house. When the heavy rain comes during the winter season, the water would rush down through the wadi and wash the sand away. The house would them come tumbling down from the power of the water rushing against the house.

Context of the Lectionary

The First Lesson. (Genesis 6:9-22, 7:24, 8:14-19) The account tells the story of faithful Noah. When God sought to destroy the people who were corrupt and disobedient, Noah with his family could survive the flood. While he was not built on a rock that could withstand the floods as in the Gospel reading, he was provided with the means to save his family and to repopulate the earth with both humans and animals. His faithfulness, even when it appeared foolish, was vindicated.

The Second Lesson. (Romans 1:16-17, 3:22b-28) The readings assert that the righteous live by faith. They are sustained not by works but by their faith which proves acceptable to God despite their sin. God provides the means for overcoming their previous sin.

Gospel. (Matthew 7:21-29) The passage brings the Sermon on the Mount to a close and prepares for the transition back to the chronology which generally follows the Gospel according to Mark.

Psalm. (Psalm 46) The Psalm expresses the trust that in the midst of all the change and distress of life, the faithful will not be shaken and brought down. Trust in God provides the believer the confidence that despite the worst that goes on around him, God is still in charge.

Content

Content of the Pericope

A. The first verses (21-23) deal with the importance of matching obedience to the will of God with a person's words of commitment.

B. The second set of verses (24-27) follow up with the importance of listening to the words which Jesus has just spoken as the foundation for life. The verb listening suggests not just the simple act of hearing but proceeding to act upon these words as the basis of life.

C. The final set of verses (28-29) stresses the reaction of the people who heard the Sermon. The authority of Jesus as one who spoke the truth is contrasted with the scribes whose teachings did not have the ring of authenticity. The issues dealt with did not address the daily concerns of the people but seemed to be pedantic.

Precis of the Parable

The parable of two foundations emphasizes the importance of hearing and doing.

A building which is not on a solid foundation is subject to external pressures. A substantial grounding in the person and teachings of Christ provides a basis for withstanding the pressures around us.

A building which has a foundation established on that which is easily attacked by outside forces is not able to persevere. Stormy events cause the building to collapse.

In like manner, a life not erected on the obedience to the words of Jesus is subject to collapse when under the pressure of forces that rage around it.

Thesis: The person who hears the words of Jesus and responds to them in action has a stability able to withstand any forces in life.

Theme: Building life on the real foundation of Christ.

Key Words of the Parable

1. "Lord, Lord." (v. 21) The term Lord in v. 21 would readily be understood in the New Testament period, both from the Hebrew and the Greek, as referring to divinity. In Hebrew usage it was a euphemism for the name of God, which was considered too holy to pronounce. If one misused the name, fearful consequences might follow. In this particular context it may have been a translation of rabbi or teacher.

2. "On that day." (v. 22) This phrase was usually understood to have eschatological reference. That is, it points to the end time when God would call all people into judgment and set up the ideal and universal kingdom at the end of the age. For samples of Old Testament uses of the phrase, see Isaiah 2:11, 17 and Zechariah 14:6.

3. "In your name." (v. 22) The name of a person was understood to represent that person's nature or essence. Thus to pray or do something "in the name of" someone was to invoke the true nature or power of that person. In some cultures people are reluctant to give their name to a stranger for fear that by knowing something of their nature the stranger will be able to exercise some power or influence over them that might do them harm or evil.

4. "Evildoers." (v. 23) The actual word translated as evildoers is *anomia*. Literally translated the word means "those who are lawless," that is, those who are without the law and therefore sinners.

5. "On the rock." (v. 24) It is not clear if the reference to the rock is only the foundation but also the whole house. Both clay and stone were used for building houses in Palestine. These materials were readily available and cheap. Apparently the building material was not of clay but of stone. Clay would be dissolved by the water of a storm or flood and be washed away. Rock would be able to withstand the assault.

6. "Wise." (v. 24) Wisdom is more than knowledge. Knowledge gives power but wisdom gives direction. In Hebrew society wisdom was seen as derived from an understanding of the law. Jesus is now proposing that wisdom comes from hearing his words or teachings and being obedient to them.

7. "Foolish." (v. 26) The foolish person is one who relies on his own knowledge and judgment without regard to the law or the will of God. Such persons do not have the ability to know the real meaning of life and the final outcome of history. They are in peril of ultimate destruction.

8. "Authority." (v. 29) Authority adheres to persons who are perceived to have knowledge, wisdom, competency, and integrity. They have no vested or personal interest in the outcome but have insight into what is real and true. Jesus was believed to have a true understanding of the meaning of life and its various relationships.

9. "Not as their scribes." (v. 29) A danger of professionalism is that one depends on book learning and tradition and loses touch with reality. Much of the teachings of the scribes of Jesus' time was involved with casuistry, which seemed to the ordinary people to be petty quibbling over minor details or rationalizations to avoid the real demands of the law. They did not seem to derive their teachings from their own experience but drew it from book learning detached from life.

Contemplation

Insights and Points to Ponder

1. Lord, Lord. Jesus objects to the kind of religion that relies only on some magical formula. People profess these magical formulas and expect that the results will come despite the absence of sufficient cause. Such formulas do not affect motivation or change behavior. True religion is more than giving verbal assent to some belief statements. Beliefs must be integrated in such a way that they lead to actions which are more than perfunctory or ceremonial. A commitment of trust in addition to belief transforms life and is manifested in actions which conform to the professions made. Someone once said that many professing Christians demonstrate by their behavior that they are practicing atheists. They act as if God does not really exist or influence their decisions and behavior.

2. Lordship. Subjection to Jesus Christ as Lord is a source of wisdom. He has a true understanding both of human nature and the moral structure of the universe. His teachings give an understanding of how persons should act to sustain a meaningful personal life and to maintain the right relationships with other people.

3. The Forces People Face. The parable suggests that the forces that assail life are external (the floods). They are in fact both outside and within a person. If persons do not prepare in advance by making commitments to real values, they will be subject to all kinds of temptations and succumb to them. They may arise from internal desires and impulses and so be within. They may also come from such external forces as persecution, peer pressures, materialism, and other false values that either attract or threaten people. While most Americans are not subject to the kinds of persecution which the first readers of Matthew's writings experienced, our pressures may be the more subtle and difficult to recognize temptations to simply fit into the society around us. We do not recognize that choices are demanded since they are not as obvious and the consequences of resisting the values of the prevailing culture are not as evident.

4. Genuine Authority. Many persons and movements claim to offer the real meaning of life. They need to be tested to see if the authority they claim is real or has only the appearance of reality. Many people are attracted to those who make strong claims to offer security or certainty. Unquestioning submission should not be given without testing what personal interest such persons or leaders of these movements have to gain. Authoritarian movements offer the attraction of certainty and remove from persons the need to make their own decisions and commitments. Eventually such authoritarian structures fail. Jesus invited persons to voluntary discipleship. He was not authoritarian in forcing people to decide. In fact, he at times discouraged too easy an acceptance and expectation of those persons who hoped to gain privilege and power by following him.

5. How do you Preach with Authority? If a preacher is to be effective, he or she must speak with authority. The danger of preaching which wins a following is that it may create a cult of personality. Those who respond may tend to worship the messenger rather than the message. A good preacher of the Gospel will point beyond to the source of the message. Persons will be invited to give allegiance, not to the messenger, but to Jesus as the Lord. Those who listen need to be reminded to test the authority to be sure that it comes from the source of the message and is not dependent upon the messenger who proclaims it.

Homily Hints

1. Building on the Rock. (7:24) Putting together the elements of a life that is built on the rock. The elements are not given magically but have to be installed through a series of behaviors until they become a reflex of character.
    A. Developing right habits
    B. Developing right attitudes
    C. Engaging in right actions

2. Testing Authority. (7:29) Persons need to test authority so as not to become dupes of the fanatics who seek power and glory for themselves and their movements.
    A. Founded in Christ
    B. Manifesting integrity through word and deed
    C. Glorifying God and not self

3. Life Founded on Sand. (7:26, 27) Consider examples of false bases for finding the meaning and welfare of life.
    A. Mind-altering and addictive drugs
    B. Sexual gratification
    C. Fame and fortune

4. Forces that Destroy or Build (7:25-27)
    A. Internal Forces arising from impulses and desires

B. External Forces arising from the environment
C. Spiritual Forces, e.g. the temptation to play God

5. Good Building Materials (7:25-27) How do we gather the materials for a good life, so that we build with stone and not the clay which dissolves before the floods that life brings?
A. Studying Scripture (good methods, proper use)
B. Prayer and meditation
C. Worship
D. The Service of Discipleship

Contact

Points of Contact

1. Independence and Dependence. A characteristic of much adolescent behavior is a shifting back and forth between independence and dependence. On the one hand, young people often rebel against parental and other authorities to gain independence and a sense of their own identity. On the other hand, they know that they always live with some dependency on others and on conditions over which they do not have control. Persons are never free from this ambiguity even as mature adults. We would like to have certainty and independence. People are particularly vulnerable to those who offer an absolute security. The prevalence of authoritarian regimes, whether political, religious, or social organizations, gives testimony to this. The parable speaks to the question of to whom obedience is given.

2. What is Genuine Worship? Worship is an acknowledgement of that which is of highest or ultimate worth. Worship that gives only verbal or token allegiance to the values represented as the object of worship is not true worship. Jesus calls for a response that goes beyond formalism. True worship transcends specific acts, times, and places. It carries over into all of life. True worship happens when that which is done on Sunday leads to actions that accord with the worthiness or values acknowledged in the formal acts as worked out throughout life.

3. A Hierarchy of Values. Some years ago a psychologist at a church-related college was trying to understand why some students persisted through four years at the college while others transferred after a year or two to another college or university. He developed the thesis that all persons have a hierarchy of values. Usually persons have some single priority or controlling value to which others are subordinated. That supreme value affects all the decisions they make. He concluded that if the person's hierarchy of values accorded with the value system embodied in the college, the student persisted and graduated from it. If it did not, the person transferred to another institution in search of one that harmonized with his or her own value system.

Jesus called disciples to accept his hierarchy of values and to act upon them. Those who were hearers *and* doers became his disciples. Others went elsewhere in search of a similar value system. A clear example would be the persons who made various excuses for not following him immediately (see Luke 9:57-62).

4. Shifting Sands. Some values seem to offer the promise of fulfillment of life. A trap of addiction which drugs offer is the promise that a person will feel good when using them. A person may try alcohol, marijuana, cocaine, or some other drug. Use of it gives a feeling of well-being. More is then used to gain the same sense of well-being. Addiction occurs when such persons cannot stand the absence of that feeling and need the drug to attain it. In many instances the frequency or size of the dose must be increased to get the same feeling or to seek a greater sense of well-being.

The drugs may come to dominate the person's life. He or she cannot live without it and will do anything to experience the feelings aroused by the drug. The person may even know that the final outcome of the drug is self-destructive. It may lead to cancer from cigarette smoking or the damage from excessive use of alcohol. It may cause the individual to become so obsessed with the drug that he or she cannot function normally. The cost and effects of the drugs may destroy family, job, income and other values in life.

Other false values also may seem to offer well-being. However, they only lead to destruction, including the pursuit of sex, money, or thrills as the goal of life. These things as a basis for a person's well-being are shifting sand. Eventually the life falls under the flood of pressures brought against it.

5. The Fads that Fail. Many fads have come and gone. They offer the promise of the answer to life. A sense of history shows the failures of these fads. Such fads in the past have been the various assurances that the world is coming to an end and that Christ will return. People who gave their lives to these promises were eventually disillusioned, sometimes with disaster for them and the movement. Nazism was a fad that captured the allegiance of a whole nation in the '30s and '40s. Communism was a longer lasting hope for many. Perhaps the New Age philosophy today is an expression of such a fad. People need to be aware of these shifting sands which prove eventually to be false and come tumbling down.

Illustrative Materials

1. The Hurricane in Florida. Prior to the hurricane that hit the area around Homestead, some builders took shortcuts. They used shoddy materials. They did not fasten the roofs securely to the superstructures of the houses. They did not use heavy enough materials for the "skin" of the houses. They did not allow sufficient structural support for the roof or the upper levels of the house. When the winds blew, the houses collapsed as though they were houses of cards.

Since the hurricane, new codes and stricter inspections have been enforced. They want to assure that any future storms of hurricane force will not cause the same extent of damage. Proven laws about proper building help assure people that the building will not fall as easily in the future.

48

2. The Absence of a Stable Foundation. In some European countries nominal church membership may be as high as 75 to 90 percent. Nevertheless, the attendance on any given Sunday outside of the high holy days, such as Christmas and Easter, may only be 2 to 3 percent. People sometimes refer to these societies as "post-Christian." They once were informed and determined largely by Christian values. Now they have become essentially secularized. They live on what has been called a "cut-flower religion." They may still have some of the appearance of the flower of Christianity in many of the social institutions and customs, but they do not have roots in the Christian faith that continue to give life to the flower. They are fading away and will eventually die if not fed by the sources of new life.

3. Loss of Authority. In recent years a number of leaders who exercised considerable authority faltered and lost their following because of their indiscretions. Jim Bakker built up the PTL Club through tele-evangelism. He had visions of a complex of institutions. They were founded on a shaky financial empire. His personal indiscretions undermined the whole structure and it came down as his authority was destroyed. Similarly Jimmy Swaggart gained a large following through his television and radio programs. His authority was destroyed when his life did not accord with what he had been preaching for others.

4. Building on Unsound Ground. Many people with plenty of money have built fancy, expensive houses on places around Los Angeles which never should have had buildings. The ground is unstable. The area has faults underneath it which makes it susceptible to earthquakes. People now say that those areas have four seasons: fire, flood, earthquake, and mud slides. Fire has denuded the ground and sometimes has taken the houses away. Heavy rain makes the ground unstable and mud slides sweep down the hills and take houses with them. Earthquakes come and destroy houses and lives. Yet people seem to be foolish enough to rebuild on the same locations!

4. Sowers Of The Seed

Matthew 13:1-9, 18-23

The same day Jesus went out of the house and sat beside the sea. ²Such great crowds gathered around him that he got into a boat and sat there, while the whole crowd stood on the beach. ³And he told them many things in parables, saying: "Listen! A sower went out to sow. ⁴And as he sowed, some seeds fell on the path, and the birds came and ate them up. ⁵Other seeds fell on rocky ground, where they did not have much soil, and they sprang up quickly, since they had no depth of soil. ⁶But when the sun rose, they were scorched; and since they had no root, they withered away. ⁷Other seeds fell among thorns, and the thorns grew up and choked them. ⁸Other seeds fell on good soil and brought forth grain, some a hundredfold, some sixty, some thirty. ⁹Let anyone with ears listen!"

¹⁸"Hear then the parable of the sower. ¹⁹When anyone hears the word of the kingdom and does not understand it, the evil one comes and snatches away what is sown in the heart; this is what was sown on the path. ²⁰As for what was sown on rocky ground, this is the one who hears the word and immediately receives it with joy; ²¹yet such a person has no root, but endures only for a while, and when trouble or persecution arises on account of the word, that person immediately falls away. ²²As for what was sown among thorns, this is the one who hears the word, but the cares of the world and the lure of wealth choke the word, and it yields nothing. ²³But as for what was sown on good soil, this is the

51

*one who hears the word and understands it, who in-
deed bears fruit and yields, in one case a hundredfold,
in another sixty, and in another thirty."*

This parable is titled "The Sower." That puts the emphasis on the person who preaches or teaches the word. Yet the parable does not do much in the way of describing the characteristics
of the sower. In this particular instance one would suppose that
Jesus implies that he is the sower. If we choose to emphasize this
aspect of the parable, then we might concentrate on the question of
how the contemporary sower corresponds to Jesus as the one who
proclaims the message.

We might also call this parable "The Seed." That would
put the emphasis on the message that is announced or communi-
cated. Again, the parable does not present any details about the
seed. No indication is given that the sower chose the seed carefully to be sure it was the best seed. The parable does not say that
the sower sifted through the grain carefully to be sure it was pure,
that no weeds or thistle seed was mixed in with the grain. If we
want to emphasize that part of the parable, then we would examine
whether the word that is sown fully represents the message that
Jesus would have us communicate.

We might also call the parable "The Soils." Indeed, that is
what is described in the passage following the parable. According
to the text, when Jesus explained the meaning of the story to his
disciples, he talked about the different kinds of soils as representing those who were receptive and responsive to the word which he
proclaimed.

Context

Context of the Church Year

The parable and the next two that follow are from Matthew 13:

Pentecost 8. Matthew 13:1-9, 18-23 — "The Sower"

Pentecost 9. Matthew 13:24-30, 36-43 — "Thistles Among
The Wheat"

Pentecost 10. Matthew 13:44-52 — "Treasure And Trash"

The parables are all concerned with the kingdom of heaven.
They present differing views of the same subject. They lend themselves well to looking at the same complex topic from different
perspectives.

Context of Matthew 13

In Matthew 13 we have another of the major teaching
sections introduced by Matthew into the general scheme of
Mark's chronology. As noted above, the central theme of the
parables is the initial message Jesus proclaimed. "The kingdom of heaven is nearby" [or "within you" or "in your midst"
— all possible meanings from the Greek.] The chapter shows
both the positive response of the disciples and the rejection of
the people of Nazareth (verses 53-58) and the Pharisees of the
earlier chapters.

Context of the Lectionary

The First Lesson. (Genesis 25:19-34) The story is of the
birth of two sons to Isaac and Rebekah. They are twin brothers but
quite different in their characteristics. They become types for the
true descendants of Abraham and the rest of the people of the world.
Even though Esau was born first and, under the rule of primogeni-
ture, should have had the inheritance, he sold it to Jacob for a mess
of stew when he was famished after a hunt.

The Second Lesson. (Romans 8:1-11) Paul asserts that
those who live by the spirit and not by the flesh continue to be
made alive by the work of the Spirit within them. The passage
contrasts the spirit and the flesh in a somewhat similar way to the
first reading where Jacob and Esau are contrasted. The passage
also relates to the parable in that the fruitful life is produced by the
action of the Spirit.

Gospel. (Matthew 13:1-9, 18-23) The parable deals with the response of hearers to the word. The latter verses are the explanation of the parable.

Psalm. (Psalm 119:105-112) The Psalmist contrasts those who live with God's word as a lamp to guide them with the wicked who are trying to trap them. Nevertheless, the faithful seek to live according to God's precepts and decrees forever. It is a prayer to be instructed so as to remain faithful.

Putting it all Together

The lessons have some commonality in the theme of productivity and faithfulness in response to God's action and the dangers from the pressures of the people around them or the temptations of the flesh.

Context of Related Scriptures

Hebrews 6:7-8 — Ground producing thorns and thistles.
2 Esdras 8:41 — Seed sown but not all fruitful.
Jeremiah 31:27 — God the sower.

Context of the Pericope

A parable generally has a single point. In some respects the parable is more of an allegory, though the main point of the parable is the consequence in the life of those who hear the message of the kingdom of heaven. The danger of allegorizing the scriptures is that persons may be led into all kinds of fanciful interpretations.

In the case of the parable, the danger is avoided by providing a controlling interpretation. The response of various persons who hear Jesus' message corresponds to the different kinds of soils on which the seed of the sower falls. Three soils are not fruitful in producing results because of the conditions of the soil.

The analogy of the various kinds of soil to different people is not perfect, since the soil is passive and people are not. The nature of the soils is given. Persons have some freedom to respond. It depends on whether people act on the seed sown (the word) or simply react to their natural state.

Thesis: 13:1-9 — Good soil brings a rich harvest of the spirit.
13:18-23 — Hearing also requires understanding.

Theme: 13:1-9 — The word has a one in four chance of succeeding in producing good fruit.
13:18-23 — Christians should be aware of obstacles to belief and avoid them.

Key Words of the Parable

1. "That same day." (v. 1) The previous two chapters deal with the attempt of the rising controversy Jesus had in response to his ministry. Still he has a popularity among the common people. Chapter 13 shifts from the controversy to Jesus' preaching to the multitudes rather than to the arguments with his opponents.

2. "The sea." (v. 1) The ministry is relocated from his hometown of Nazareth to the area around the north shore of the Sea of Galilee, now called Lake Tiberias.

3. "Listen!" (v. 3) Other versions translate the term as "Behold." It is an attention-getting device. Jesus, in a boat with a multitude of people scattered along the shore, needed some way to bring the crowd to focus. Experts on communications talk about the need to provide a "hook" at the beginning of a message. We need that admonition also.

4. "Sowing." (vv. 4-7) In Palestine the method of sowing was different from what is known in industrialized countries today. The persons planting seeds used the broadcast method. They walked along a strip, scattering the seed from a bag slung over the shoulder and hanging at about waist level. As they finished the strip, they went back and plowed it to mix the seed into the soil. In some instances two persons worked together, one scattering the seed and the other following with the plow. In this way the soil on which the seed might be lodged was somewhat haphazard and the seed might be cast on different kinds of soil.

5. "On the path." (v. 4) People and animals tend to follow well-worn tracks. They choose either the most direct or easy way to their goal. The earth then gets compacted as they traverse the same path. The seeds would lie on the top of the ground and be readily visible to birds who would eat them.

6. "Rocky ground." (v. 5) In Palestine the soil is often a very thin layer over a sub-strata of rocks. Without the deep plowing that is possible with modern metal plows, the sower would not know that a particular spot had rocks close to the surface. The roots would have no depth and little moisture, so the plant would wither and die under the blazing sun.

7. "Thorns." (v. 7) The cultivation of the soil on agricultural land in Palestine did not go deep enough to remove the roots of thistles and thorns. Seed planted would not grow up fast enough to get ahead of thistles and thorns which started from roots and not seeds. Some of these plants grow to the height of five or six feet and could strangle the grain.

8. "Some hundredfold, some sixty, some thirty." (v. 8) Such return would be an unusually rich harvest. The average productivity in the United States is about thirtyfold, even with advanced agriculture, including hybrid seeds, mechanical plowing and planting, and the use of fertilizers.

9. "Ears." (v. 9) The important thing is not just hearing the sound of words. The more important thing is to understand and obey the meaning of the words. They need to be translated into life and action.

10. "Kingdom." (v. 18) While the kingdom has a future fulfillment, it is already present in the spiritual community. It has God as the sovereign Lord and Christ as its head. It is realized wherever the church is living in obedience to God as king.

11. "Trouble or persecution." (v. 21) Some raise the question as to whether this phrase is anticipation of what is to come or is a later addition by the church at the time Matthew or Mark wrote their gospel accounts. In any event it is a warning against the danger of falling away when opposition comes.

Contemplation

Insights

1. Our Responsibilities as Sower. If we sow the seed of the word, we may have some concern about where it is deposited. The main responsibility for creating the results lies with the Holy Spirit at work in those who listen, but we must do the best in our ability to make the word understood. Jesus used parables so that people would remember the story even if they did not immediately grasp its application. Later at an appropriate time it might hit home with them.

2. The Harvest of Fruit. Our concern should not be how great the harvest of fruit is, to get caught in the numbers game as the only measure of successful activity. Rather it is that there is some harvest, whether thirty, sixty, or one hundredfold. Invidious comparisons among Christians or Christian groups should not be made in terms of the amount of fruit (growth) produced. It should rather be that we are faithful "sowers of the seed."

3. The Central Point of the Parable. The central point of the parable should grant hope. The Holy Spirit will not leave the word devoid of results. We should not be too disturbed about the kind of soil in which we sow the word. Some of it will produce results, not so much because of our doing, but because the soil is receptive already.

4. Sowing the Seed Prolifically. The sower is not stingy in sowing the seed. The sower continued to sow even where it did not appear to be productive of fruit. The opportunity ought to be offered to respond and be fruitful.

5. The Seed is the Word. A Christian is a person who is born again. The word, both spoken and acted, is the seed that activates the process that leads to a new birth. Those who teach and preach are servants of the word. They plant the seed but it takes time for it to germinate and develop until it produces the fruit of the new life in Christ.

Homily Hints

1. A Variety of Soils. What are the various personality types who respond to the word proclaimed?
   A. The Overly Intellectual. Persons such as Nicodemus in John 3 are too prosaic. They include the bigot who has a closed mind, or the person who cannot see any truth to the spiritual realm beyond the physical and material.
   B. The Overly Emotional. Some people respond quickly and easily to every appeal. They quickly flit from one interest to another which moves them at the moment.
   C. The Defective Will. These are led by their desires. They are distracted by the pursuit of pleasures, fame, or wealth. They have a low frustration level so that they cannot stand any deferred reward. They make no persistent commitment to anything beyond themselves.
   D. The Receptive Mind. People who have a balance of head, heart, and backbone consult all their powers. They make a commitment to the reality which fulfills their total personality.

2. Cultivating the Soil. While the parable does not discuss the way in which the soil can be prepared, cultivating the soil can be helpful in allowing the seed to take root.

A. Watering the Soil. It has been said that you can lead a horse to water, but you can't make it drink. Someone has suggested that you can put salt in the water. People often know only their wants and not their needs. Making them conscious of the need may help.

B. Fertilizing the Soil. Adding examples of the productive life may help persons to be enriched by following them and enriching their lives.

C. Sunlight Needed. Light needs to be shed to overcome the negative effects of the darkness in the world.

3. The Power of Preaching.
A. Depends on the Quality of the Seed.
B. Depends on the Nature of the Soil.
C. The Results are the Fruits of the Spirit.

4. The Perils of Prosperity.
A. The Illusion of Self-sufficiency.
B. The Attraction of Wealth.
C. The Necessity that Truth be Tested.

5. The Fruitful Life. How does the seed of the word affect our behavior in various areas of life?
A. In Personal Life.
B. In Social Life.
C. In Spiritual Life.

Contact

Points of Contact

1. Barriers to Communication. Preaching and teaching are about communication. For successful communication, both a sender and receiver are required. Often "static" interferes between the sender and receiver so that the message does not get through. People may be preoccupied with some personal problem that prevents them from listening. People who are hungry or on drugs cannot hear because of their internal state. The actions of the sender may belie the message that is being sent. If no integrity exists between the message being sent and the action of the sender, the wrong message may get through to the receiver. Talking over the heads of people is not a sign of erudition, but of poor aim with the message. With an increasing aging population, more people have problems hearing. Frequently among the older people, one hears them say, "I could not understand a word he said!" Jesus knew his audience and addressed them where they were.

2. The Need for Active Listening. It is part of the responsibility of hearers to interact with the speaker. They need to be aroused so that they do not listen passively, but ask themselves: What does this mean for me, how does it apply to my life situation, what changes do I need to make? A good listening congregation can draw the best out of a preacher or teacher.

3. A Cross-cultural Sowing. The sower does not take full responsibility for the kind of fruit resulting from the seed. In times past, persons engaged in sowing the seed in cultures other than their own often too easily identified the form of their culture with the substance of the message. Increasingly it is recognized that the seed must be sown so that persons know the central message of the kingdom. The forms which it takes should be allowed to emerge as the persons apply the message in their own time and place, rather than in some preconceived essential cultural form.

Points to Ponder

1. How much responsibility do we take for the soil? Do we too easily assume that the only place and time for presenting the message of the kingdom is in a church building at a traditional time? Do we need to find ways to reach people at a time and place more convenient to them? Jesus met the multitudes, not in the synagogue or temple only, or on the sabbath only. He preached from a boat on the seashore when the multitudes met him there. He went out of the house and did not wait for the people to come to him (see vv. 1-3).

2. The Holy Spirit's Action. When do we become too anxious about the harvest that must come from our preaching? In some Moslem cultures, more dead missionaries are buried than live Christians are found. How long does one labor and sow in waiting for the Holy Spirit to fructify our work?

Illustrative Materials

1. Strangeness of Seed Sprouting. Sometimes the word given has surprising results. Once in speaking to two young men, a person was trying to convince one of them to consider a college and seminary preparation with possibility of entering the ministry. He assumed that only one of the two showed such promise. Interestingly enough, the person addressed enrolled at college, but left after a very short time and never completed college. The other, in part because of the conversation, came to the college, went to seminary, and prepared for the ministry.

2. The Uncertainty of Return. Someone once pointed out the low return for Jesus among his disciples. One betrayed him. Only three seemed to be closely related to him during his lifetime. Not many of the disciples were prominent in the early church. So that his "batting average" with the disciples was not high, but for those who responded, the results were amazing.

3. Sponges. If we change the image from soils and seeds, we might suggest that some hearers are like sponges. They may absorb the message given, but they have to be pressed to give up to others what has been received.

4. Results Exceeding the Sower. Teachers often find that their students go on to do greater and better things than the teachers were ever able to accomplish personally. It is gratifying to have students who are prodded or inspired to go on to greater heights than might have been expected when they were students.

5. Planting Seeds Early in Life. In Russia attempts were made for more than two generations to eliminate Christianity. It was eliminated from the schools, attacked and discouraged. The society was officially atheist. The *babushkas* (usually grandmothers of children) took care of the children because both parents worked. They shared with the grandchildren their faith. Thus Christianity was not eliminated and since the collapse of the Soviet Union is making a remarkable comeback. The churches are full and a great demand exists for Bibles. It is probably no accident that Gorbachev, who started the reform, was baptized as a child. Seed was planted early and later bore fruit.

5. Thistles Among The Wheat

Matthew 13:24-30, 36-43

He put before them another parable: "The kingdom of heaven may be compared to someone who sowed good seed in his field; ²⁵but while everyone was asleep, an enemy came and sowed weeds among the wheat, and then went away. ²⁶So when the plants came up and bore grain, then the weeds appeared as well. ²⁷And the slaves of the householder came and said to him, 'Master, did you not sow good seed in your field? Where, then, did these weeds come from?' ²⁸He answered, 'An enemy has done this.' The slaves said to him, 'Then do you want us to go and gather them?' ²⁹But he replied, 'No; for in gathering the weeds you would uproot the wheat along with them. ³⁰Let both of them grow together until the harvest; and at harvest time I will tell the reapers, Collect the weeds first and bind them in bundles to be burned, but gather the wheat into my barn.'"

³⁶Then he left the crowds and went into the house. And his disciples approached him, saying, "Explain to us the parable of the weeds of the field." ³⁷He answered, "The one who sows the good seed is the Son of Man; ³⁸the field is the world, and the good seed are the children of the kingdom; the weeds are the children of the evil one, ³⁹and the enemy who sowed them is the devil; the harvest is the end of the age, and the reapers are angels. ⁴⁰Just as the weeds are collected and burned up with fire, so will it be at the end of the age. ⁴¹The Son of Man will send his angels, and they will collect

out of his kingdom all causes of sin and all evildoers,
[42]and they will throw them into the furnace of fire, where
there will be weeping and gnashing of teeth. [43]Then
the righteous will shine like the sun in the kingdom of
their Father. Let anyone with ears listen!"

The parable of the weeds and wheat is intriguing. It raises a number of issues that are complex and can be confusing. Some resolutions of the issues are suggested while for others you need to look elsewhere for more adequate explanations. Some differences are found within the parable itself and the interpretation given to the disciples.

One of the issues is the question about the nature of the church. Does this parable apply to the church as part of the kingdom of God? If so, is the church a divine or a human institution? How should the church deal with differences and dissent among its members? Should a person ever be excluded from membership in the church? What kind, if any, of discipline should the church exercise? If so, when, why and how? Is the church intended to be inclusive so that it encompasses anyone who wants to belong? Or is the church exclusive, so that certain conditions are established for entrance into and continuing in membership in the church? It is the issue posed by Troeltsch in his description of the church as inclusive or the sect as exclusive. Which should be the true form of the church?

Another broad issue raised by the interpretation of the parable is the presence of evil in the church and in the world. Should the church advocate the eradication of the evil by destroying the perpetrators of evil? What is the role of the church in supporting attempts to remove the evil? It even raises the question of why a good and powerful God permits evil to persist in the world. Can we trust that God will ultimately overcome all evil? If so, when and how will that happen? How should the church and Christians behave toward the evil in the world during the interim until God brings the end of history, especially when evil seems to be overwhelming the good?

Context

The parable is one of three in the current series, all having a similar purpose in understanding the nature of the kingdom of heaven.

Context of Matthew 13

Three parables from an agricultural setting are given in succession in Matthew 13: the parable of the seeds and the sower for the previous Sunday, the parable of the weeds and wheat for this Sunday, and the parable of the mustard seed which interrupts the flow from this Sunday's parable and its interpretation in verses 36-43. Three additional parables are found in Matthew 13. They will be the Gospel reading for Pentecost 10.

Context of the Lectionary Lesson

The First Lesson. (Genesis 28:10-19a) Jacob is in flight after having tricked his brother Esau into giving him the inheritance in exchange for a mess of pottage. As he sleeps at night he has a dream of God's messengers ascending and descending from heaven. In the dream he gains assurance that he is in the line of Abraham and will be the recipient of the promise of his covenant. When he awakes he memorializes the place and calls it Bethel, the house of God.

The Second Lesson. (Romans 8:12-25) This lesson deals with the universal need for deliverance from sin. Those who accept God's deliverance will be his heirs. The Gospel account waits for the harvest. This passage waits with hope for a full deliverance of all creation.

Gospel. (Matthew 13:24-30; 36-43) The parable uses a story about weeds in the midst of wheat and Jesus' interpretation of it to the disciples. He deals with the issue of evil in the midst of the world and the church. It addresses God's prerogative in dealing with the eventual elimination of the evil.

Psalm. (Psalm 139:1-12, 23-24) The psalmist acknowledges that nothing can be kept hidden from God. God knows our innermost being. Though Jacob could flee from his brother Esau in the first lesson, the psalmist asserts that it is not possible to flee from God. Jacob in his flight also did not escape from God's presence. The psalmist concludes by praying for God to examine him and to lead him in the way everlasting.

Context of Related Scriptures

> Daniel 12:3 — An earlier use of the expression "then the righteous will shine."
> 2 Esdras 7:36 — Mention of the furnace of fire.
> Matthew 3:12 — Another instance of gathering the wheat into the granary and winnowing the chaff with fire.
> Matthew 18:15-20 — The process for dealing with sin within the church.
> Matthew 28:20 — A favorite phrase of Matthew about "the end of the age."
> Mark 4:26-29 — Has some parallel ideas of wheat growing and harvested, but without the weeds growing in the midst.

Precis of the Parable

The parable tells of an incident that would be familiar to those who heard it. In a society which was basically rural and agriculturally related in character, the growth of weeds in the midst of a grain field would be common. Weeds growing in a field of wheat can still be seen where farmers do not use herbicides.

Some commentators raise the question as to whether the parable is a variant of the parable recorded in Mark 4:26-29 since the parable only appears in Matthew. In Mark's parable the point is that God gives the increase which results in a fruitful harvest. Perhaps Matthew expanded on the parable to explain the experience of the early church when it became evident that not everyone in the church acted purely.

A somewhat different emphasis is given in the interpretation in verses 36 to 43. Many commentators are inclined to believe that this interpretation did not come from Jesus. It seems to have more linguistic characteristics from Matthew than from the sayings of Jesus recorded elsewhere. The commentators speculate that the interpretation which seems to shift the locus of the field from the church to the world and introduces a second sower who accounts for the weeds as a deliberate act represents the experience of the later church.

Thesis: God is the judge of what is ultimately good and evil.

Theme: The experience of evil and good in history is ambiguous. Human perceptions of what is real and what appears as evil are not certain.

Key Words of the Parable

1. "Asleep." (v. 25) This term may be an echo of Mark 4:27. In both instances the growth took place while persons slept, so they cannot take full credit for the harvest. In the final analysis it is the work of God.

2. "Enemy." (v. 25) The interpretation in v. 39 describes the enemy as the devil.

3. "Weeds." (v. 25) The weeds were *darnel (lolium termulentum)*. When they grew up they had a similar appearance to wheat, though they were slightly darker in color. They did grow as tall as wheat. Their seed was poisonous. Rabbis considered them as a perverted form of wheat.

4. "Slaves." (v. 28) Probably the disciples if from Jesus, or, if from Matthew, others in the later church who wanted to purge the church of all whom they considered unfaithful.

67

5. "Let them grow together." (v. 30) This is the main point of the parable. It calls for a measure of tolerance for sinners in the church, and later, as part of the interpretation, in the world.

6. "Weeds first and bind them in bundles to be burned." (v. 30) An image of the last judgment. God had promised after the Noah experience not to destroy the world by flood. In the New Testament period, the final judgment was anticipated to be accompanied with destruction by fire. See, for example, 2 Peter 3:11-13.

7. "Then he left the crowds." (v. 36) The interpretation was not given to the multitudes but only to the inner circle of disciples.

8. "The Son of Man." (v. 37) The term sometimes referred simply to a person when used with the indefinite article, "a son of man." In this case where the definitive article was used, it denotes the title of the apocalyptic figure associated with the final outcome of history.

9. "The field." (v. 38) The figure is of a global nature, not the "world" as sometimes used in a missionary sense.

10. "Children of the evil one." (v. 38) Some commentators think this is a harsh judgment of the Jews.

11. "Evildoers." (v. 41) Literally from the Greek "doers of lawlessness."

12. "Weeping and gnashing of teeth." (v. 42) Except for a use in Luke 13:28, the phrase seems to be used only in Matthew. It appears elsewhere in Matthew 13:50, 22:13, 24:51, and 25:30, always as a transhistorical event.

Contemplation

Insights

1. The Age of Redemption vs. Judgment. Jesus came as an agent of redemption. His message was one of repentance, grace, and forgiveness. Only at the "end of the age" would Christ be an agent of judgment. Now in history is the opportunity to avert the consequences of judgment and to prepare to participate in the full glory of the heavenly kingdom when it is revealed in its fullness.

2. The Way of Invitation. The method Jesus used and to which he called his disciples was that of inviting all people to enter the kingdom of heaven. It is not the way of coercion, forceful conversion, or the destruction of those who decline the invitation or oppose the kingdom. Instead it is to woo them by the attractive power of the kingdom and to warn them of the death to which they are tending when they refuse the invitation.

3. Confidence in the outcome of history. The parable manifests a confidence about the working of God's kingdom in history. If the seed is sown, we can be confident that it will germinate without our having to force it. It will produce fruit and the harvest will come. We are not the servants who are to try to sort out the ambiguities of good and evil in history. Rather we are to sow the seed and wait in confidence that the harvest will come, that the good will endure beyond the fruits of evil.

4. Evil is found in the world. Dante in his *Divine Comedy* says the evil is an absence, excess, or distortion of a good. In a world created by God anything that is absolutely or totally evil could not be allowed to exist. Nevertheless, evil is real and we need to contend with it. We need to recover the good intended by the Creator from the evil. In the world and in history, evil exists and we need to participate both in the struggle to overcome it and to discover the good that lies beyond the evil. We do so in the faith that the good is more enduring than the evil because God is both good and powerful.

5. The Field is the World. "America: Love it or Leave it," "They ought to go back where they came from" and "Yankee go home" are slogans often heard when persons do not agree with someone who speaks out against an injustice or an evil. The kingdom of heaven is not restricted by political boundaries set up by human institutions. The call to sow the seed is to go into all the world, to all of God's creation. It is all God's domain, and if we are members of his kingdom and are to sow the seed in faithfulness, our vision and our terrain is global in reach.

Homily Hints

1. Hope of Harvest. The parable offers an opportunity to consider the evangelism process, whether it is within the church family or as a mission outreach.

    A. The Seed is Sown. What is the message of the gospel that needs to be given to people?

    B. The Seed Grows. How does the church nurture the seed, but how do you let it happen without intervention?

    C. The Harvest Comes. To what degree does the church screen out who becomes members and to what degree does the church accept members with the final judgment in God's hands?

2. The Kingdom Conquers Evil. People need hope in facing the mixture of good and evil.

    A. Evils in the World.

    B. Good in the World.

    C. God Assures the Greater Good.

3. Evil is Self-Destructive. Here deal with why we should participate in the good and refrain from the evil.

    A. Evil is Counteractive. Evil has no center of energy, no organizing principle. Instead, various evils act against each other in chaos that is self-destructive.

B. Good is Cumulative. Because God gives a center to good actions, they reinforce each other in a harmony of order. This means the power of a good increases the power of other goods and then in turn is increased by them also.

C. History Moves Toward Good Ends. Despite the apparently overwhelming evils of the moment, evil is transitory; only the good persists.

4. The Church's Responsibility for the World.

A. When are we Responsible for the World?

B. When do we Leave the World to God?

C. Tolerance for Some Mix of Good and Evil.

5. The Deceptive Nature of Evil. Just as the weeds at times look like wheat, so some evils are attractive because they look like a good.

A. The Deceptive Nature of Drugs. Why do people think drugs are good? What are the misleading aspects of them?

B. The Deception of Sex. Why is something as good as sex and as necessary for the future of the race so wrong when practiced promiscuously?

C. The Deception of Wealth. When does the pursuit of wealth become an evil?

Contact

Points of Contact

1. The Weeds in the Christian. We all have biological urges which help to maintain life and make us survivors. Yet the greatest good can become a great evil. For example, the sexual drive which helps to assure the survival of the race can lead to the most intimate and loving relationship between two people and lead to a caring, nurturing family. Yet the abuse of sex can lead to the most bitter relationships if fulfillment of the drive is perverted or abused. Crimes of passion are some of the most tragic.

71

2. Weeds in the World. A frequent puzzle for people is why good does not always seem to happen to people of faith while others seem to escape unscathed. People ask, why do I or a loved one suffer an incurable disease or a fatal accident? They need to prepare for the suffering of disease or a natural disaster, not only at the time when it occurs, but ahead of such events.

3. The Mystery of Growth. In the spring of the year what appears to be dead comes to new life. The work of the Holy Spirit operates in a similar way in the life of people. It is always something of a mystery as to how and when people are aroused to faith. We can work at teaching and preaching, yet people do not automatically respond. It is often surprising when some people seem suddenly to respond and begin to show unexpected promise.

4. The Illusion of Good and Evil. Our judgments of people can be fallible. Our knowledge of how people turn out and what brings change is faulty. Who would have thought that Saul when persecuting the church would become Paul, the greatest missionary in spreading the church to the Gentile world and leaving a body of literature to guide the church for future generations? If we call for the death of some person because of the appearance of evil, how do we know whether we will prevent the ministry of a significant agent for accomplishing God's will? We need a tolerance for the growth of the weeds and the wheat together because we cannot always know in the final analysis which is which.

Points to Ponder

1. Church Discipline. When, why, and how does the church exercise discipline? Three reasons are often given for disciplining church members: 1. To redeem the sinners. 2. To keep the church from being infected by the example of the sinner. 3. To protect the reputation of the church in the world. If the prime reasons become two and three instead of one, discipline easily becomes punitive instead of redemptive. If no discipline is exercised, it appears that the church is indifferent toward sin. How do

72

you maintain the purity of the church and still allow for that sin that befalls all of us at times?

2. What are the Limits of Means to Oppose Evil? Are some means of eliminating evil also evil? Can we ever use evil means to cast out evil? When do we become guilty of playing God if we try to eradicate evil by destroying the evildoer? Do we leave the outcome of evil in history in God's hands, or do we take some actions against evil, but refrain from seeking final solutions to evil in history? When do we set bounds on our actions and leave the harvest to God's wisdom and power?

3. Are the Weeds Only in the World? Does the parable only have reference to how we deal with sin inside the church, or does it have reference to the world and the church? If it only has reference to the church, or both to the world and the church, what are the implications for the actions of the church in toleration of the mixture of weeds and wheat?

4. Our Mission to the World. To what extent should Christians be involved in trying to deal with evil in the world? Should the church be engaged in social action: solving problems of unemployment, homelessness, crime prevention, drug addiction, overpopulation, and similar issues? Is the church concerned about the amelioration of evil by minimizing violence, correcting violations of human rights, eliminating injustice, and working to avoid environmental degradation? Or is it the church's task only to preach the gospel and seek the conversion of persons, and to leave the problems of society to other agencies? Is social change a hopeless endeavor since evil and sin will continue to exist along with the good in history?

5. Heresy and Dissent. What is the role of heresy and dissent in clarifying truth? Have not the disagreements of the past helped the church to arrive at a better understanding of Christian doctrine? How do we deal with heresies to use them constructively for the faith and not destructively?

1. The Seed of the Word. Including New Testaments, booklets and tracts, the American Bible Society (ABS) reported that it distributed 15,000 pieces to those who survived the midwestern floods of 1993. They were active from North Dakota to Missouri, supporting church groups, disaster relief agencies, the Salvation Army and community groups. The ABS also distributed 21,000 pieces after the January 1994, Los Angeles earthquake.

2. Planting the Seed. In 1994 permission was granted to evangelical Christians in Iraq to organize Bible studies in the public schools. The Ministry of Religion also arranged with the Bible League to receive materials. According to *The Church and The World*, 2,000 Bibles were recently shipped to local churches.

3. Eradicating Weeds. In the sixteenth century in the Netherlands, a church dispute arose. As it became increasingly severe, two groups separated with each excommunicating the other. An issue to be settled was the use of the substantial church building. The two groups finally agreed to build a wall down the center of the sanctuary. Both parties continued to worship in the building, but a wall separated them!

4. Separating Weeds and Wheat. Some church groups have sought to keep a pure church by excommunicating those with whom they do not agree. In one instance it went to such an extreme that a leader excommunicated everyone but himself and his wife.

5. A Bad Harvest. In the Middle Ages the Spanish Inquisition tried desperately to root out all heresy. Many persons were burned at the stake in so-called *auto-de-fe*s. Some historians have proposed that after the Inquisition executed many of the best people the impoverishment of Spain lasted for centuries and that accounts for its slow progress into a modern society.

6. Planting Thistles. "The Meanest Man"

He carried thistle seeds in his pocket,
and now and then dropped some on favorable ground —
favorable, that is, to his personal dislikes —
and pushed them in with his heel.[1]

7. Choosing the Right Seed. On July 29, 1994, a former Presbyterian pastor, Paul Jennings Hill, shot abortion doctor John Bayard Britton and his escort Herman Barrett and wounded Barrett's wife June in the arm in Pensacola, Florida. A later report indicated that Paul Hill was in part influenced in his action by the Rev. David Trosch, a Catholic priest who was removed from his parish by Mobile Archbishop Oscar Lipscomb because he was advocating the slaying of abortion doctors. The priest owns two guns, a .22 pistol and a .20 gauge shotgun. He has never used them to kill anything other than a bird on one occasion. The report said, however, that he has weapons that may be a graver danger than his guns: that is, his mouth and his clerical collar. The Rev. Trosch earlier had paid to advertise a cartoon that showed an anti-abortionist shooting an abortion doctor with the caption "Justifiable Homicide." The Rev. Trosch is known to have been friendly with Paul Hill after the earlier shooting of another doctor in Pensacola. Some would hold Trosch equally responsible for the deaths of Dr. Britton and Herman Barrett and the wounding of June Barrett.

---

[1]Millen Brand, *Local Lives*, (New York: Clarkson N. Potter, Inc., 1975), p. 334.

6. Treasures And Trash

Matthew 13:44-52

"The kingdom of heaven is like treasure hidden in a field, which someone found and hid; then in his joy he goes and sells all that he has and buys that field.

45"Again, the kingdom of heaven is like a merchant in search of fine pearls; 46on finding one pearl of great value, he went and sold all that he had and bought it.

47"Again, the kingdom of heaven is like a net that was thrown into the sea and caught fish of every kind; 48when it was full, they drew it ashore, sat down, and put the good into baskets but threw out the bad. 49So it will be at the end of the age. The angels will come out and separate the evil from the righteous, 50and throw them into the furnace of fire, where there will be weeping and gnashing of teeth.

51"Have you understood all this?" They answered, "Yes." 52And he said to them, "Therefore every scribe who has been trained for the kingdom of heaven is like the master of a household who brings out of his treasure what is new and what is old."

The parables in Matthew 13:44-52 continue the series of eight that are found in this chapter. The previous parables were told in public to a large crowd (see Matthew 13:1-3). Now Jesus moves into a house where the disciples came to him (Matthew 13:36). He first explains the parable about the weeds among the wheat. He then proceeds to tell the three parables in Matthew 13:44-52. Two of the parables, the treasure hidden in the field and the pearl of great value, are twins. The third parable about the net and fishes is a twin to the earlier parable about the weeds and the wheat. This follows a familiar organizing principle in Matthew of ABBA. Again all three parables are intended to describe the nature and value of the kingdom of heaven. They all begin with the same phrase, "the kingdom of heaven is like ..." The section ends with a summary statement addressed to the disciples who are compared to scribes.

Context

The parables are for the tenth Sunday following Pentecost and conclude a series of three Sundays dealing with the parables of the kingdom from Matthew 13.

Context of the Lectionary

The First Lesson. (Genesis 29:15-28) The story of Jacob continues from last week. He is now working for Laban. The trickster who tricked his brother out of his inheritance is in turn tricked into marrying Leah instead of Rachel. He had to work another seven years before he finally was granted Rachel as his wife.

The Second Lesson. (Romans 8:26-39) The first half of this reading gives assurance of support by the Spirit. The second half gives further assurance that all things work together for good for those who are called by God. It is one of the key passages that raises the difficult issue of predestination. It ends with the assertion that nothing in all the world can separate the faithful from the love of God.

Gospel. (Matthew 13:31-33, 44-52) The reading brings to a conclusion the three-week series of parables followed from Matthew 13.

Psalm. (Psalm 105:1-11, 45b) The Psalm connects the seeking of the second parable in today's gospel reading about the pearl of great value. It also relates back to the God of Abraham, Isaac and Jacob with the promise of the holy land given to Moses in the first lesson for today. It ends with an exclamation of praise to the Lord.

Context of Related Scripture

> Leviticus 11:9-12 — Description of clean and unclean fish.
> Job 19:6 — Closed into a net by God.
> Job 28:18 — "The price of wisdom is above pearls."
> Psalm 66:11 — Use of the image of the net into which we are drawn.
> Ecclesiastes 9:12 — Image of fish caught into a cruel net compared with mortals snared by calamity.
> Habakkuk 1:15-17 — An opposing view of the net as used by the enemy.
> Matthew 6:19-21 — (Luke 12:33-34) — Treasures on earth or heaven.
> Matthew 6:33 — Seeking first the kingdom.
> Matthew 7:6 — Throwing pearls before swine.
> Matthew 25:14-30 — Note that one of the servants buried a talent in the earth for safe keeping.
> Revelation 22:21 — Each of the 12 gates are made from a single pearl.

Content

The first two parables are more similes than parables. They do not provide many details. Nothing is said about the amount of the treasure in the first instance. It is assumed that the treasure is of considerable size. In the second parable nothing is said about why the person would want to possess the pearl. Was the merchant wanting to sell it again and gain a great profit? Or did he want it as a source of status and pride of possession? These kinds of questions were not of concern in telling the story. The main point of each is the good fortune that each had in discovering the treasure and the price they were willing to pay to possess them.

Some contrasts can be noted between the first two parables. In the treasure hidden in the field, the person who found the treasure was probably poor. He had to sell all that he had to purchase the field. The person in the parable of the costly pearl apparently was of some wealth since he could afford to travel to find the pearl.

A second contrast is between the accidental finding of the treasure in the field as opposed to the merchant who went searching for the beautiful pearl. A third contrast is between the presumed multiple nature of the treasure in a box as opposed to the unitary nature of the pearl.

The third parable would particularly speak to the disciples who were fishermen. They no doubt had often sat on the shore of Galilee and sorted out their catch of fish. They would cast aside the fish which were considered unclean by the Levitical law. This parable is very similar to the parable of the weeds in the wheat in that the good and the bad were mixed together, the weeds in the field of wheat and the good and bad fish in the sea. They both have the element of harvest before the good and the bad were separated. They both have as their main point the implied warning of the fate of the bad as opposed to the fate of the good.

The final verses of the section offer a summary statement of the entire chapter. Matthew earlier had contrasted what was said from the old tradition with what Jesus said as fulfillment of the intention but which became a new statement of the principles. It is not entirely clear exactly what the reference to the old and the new is. The most general understanding would be the old as the Law and the new as the Gospel. It could also be the old as representing the human kingdom of Israel which was bound by geography and ethnicity while the new is the spiritual kingdom that is universal in scope and no longer bound by the particularity of time and place.

Precis of the Parables

The emphasis of the twin parables is on the joy at the good fortune of those who find the kingdom. All other treasures that persons find of value are to be sacrificed to obtain the much greater value of the kingdom. The third parable underscores the same point as the previous parable of the weeds in the wheat. At the end of history a sorting takes place between good and evil. Only the good eventually survives and endures. The final verse suggests that the disciples retain the values which they had received from Judaism. They are also to understand the new interpretations and teachings which came from Jesus.

Thesis: The incomparable worth of the kingdom of heaven.

Theme: The kingdom is worth any cost.

Key Words in the Parables

1. "Heaven." (v. 44) Matthew uses the term *the kingdom of heaven* where Luke speaks of the kingdom of God. The difference reflects the cultural background of the two writers. Matthew comes from a Hebrew background. He would be reluctant to use the name of God. In the Old Testament, it was the name written but not pronounced. The term *heaven* is a euphemism to avoid the danger of profaning the name of God. Luke had a gentile background. He would not have the same hesitation as Matthew.

2. "Hidden in a field." (v. 44) In biblical times no one had banks which were a secure place to deposit wealth. Houses also were not safe places to keep a treasure. Especially in times of chaos, such as war, people would bury their gold, silver, jewels, and other precious items which were durable in the ground. Subsequently, they might be killed or exiled and the knowledge of the location of the hidden treasure was lost. At a later time someone might stumble upon the treasure and recover it.

"3. Found ... hid." (v. 44) We might raise the ethical issue of finding a treasure in a field that did not belong to us and then hiding it so we can purchase the field. Buying the field without disclosing the true value of the field containing the treasure is a form of deception. While the ethics might be questionable, it was

81

legal to do so at that time. An unclaimed hidden treasure became the property of the owner of the place where it was located. The law presumed that the seller of the field was not the owner of the treasure or he would not sell it at a price much less than it was worth. The principle was somewhat like the saying, "Finders keepers, losers weepers!"

4. **"A merchant."** (v. 45) Pearls were not usually found in Palestine. A merchant might travel to the Red Sea, the Persian Gulf, or even to the Indian Ocean in search of pearls.

5. **"Pearl."** (v. 45) A pearl was a scarce item. It held a place in the society of the time that diamonds hold in our society. Pearls could be used as currency. To serve as currency for trade, anything has to have certain properties. It has to be relatively scarce to make it desirable. It has to be stable so that it will not easily diminish in value over time. And it has to be small enough to be easily portable. Pearls met all of these requirements.

6. **"Net."** (v. 47) The net used would be a dragnet. It was sometimes attached on shore at one end and then drug by the boat out into the water to surround and catch the fish. At other times two boats were used to drag the net in a large circle and catch all the fish in a given area.

7. **"Fish of every kind."** (v. 47) It is not clear whether Jesus deliberately intended to include every kind of fish in the world and thereby to imply the universality of his message. He may have intended to imply that the kingdom of heaven did not just include the Jews. According to some sources, at the time they thought all the different kinds of fish in the world numbered 153.

8. **"When it was full."** (v. 48) This expression points to the end of history, the time of fulfillment. At that time judgment will be made.

9. **"Threw out the bad."** (v. 48) According to Levitical law

only fish that had scales and fins were edible. People were not to eat any swarming creatures in the water which did not have fins and scales. They were detested.

10. "Scribes ... trained for the kingdom ..." (v. 52) The disciples were to be learners. They had to be experts about the nature of the kingdom of heaven as opposed to the scribes of the Pharisees who were experts in the law. Some raise the question as to whether at the time that Matthew wrote scribes were a functioning position in the Christian church or not.

Contemplation

Insights

1. The Message of Joy. The person who found the treasure in the field responded with joy at his discovery. Jesus frequently participated in the joys of life. He attended weddings. He enjoyed banquets. He found stimulating conversation in the home of Mary and Martha. He attended a wedding. These activities were quite a contrast to John the Baptist who lived a very ascetic and probably lonely life in the desert. His was a message of doom. Jesus, on the other hand, generally invited people to the heavenly banquet. While those who came to John the Baptist might be scared into repentance, those who followed Jesus were attracted by his love. A Christian church which is an evangelistic church will attract people by the joy manifested in the life of the members who have discovered love, joy, and peace in Christ.

2. The Highest Good. Often the enemy of the highest good is the satisfaction with a lesser good. The merchant who searched for the pearl of great value was restless with lesser values. In a sense, human beings are never fully satisfied that they have achieved their full potential. The Christian life is a constant striving for complete fulfillment of possibilities. Christians are drawn by the high example given in Jesus Christ. They can constantly grow into the fullest maturity but they do so without the pervasive anxiety of those who have the underlying feeling, consciously or unconsciously, that they have missed the real meaning of life.

3. Paying the Price. Note that neither the man who bought the field nor the merchant had any hesitation or showed any regrets in having to pay the price to acquire the treasure and the pearl. Some Christians give the impression that they have made a great sacrifice in becoming Christian. They have given up "worldly pleasures" which have no enduring value. It is life in the kingdom that gives real pleasure and satisfaction. It is not fleeting and momentary but deep and lasting, if they have found the love of Christ filling their lives and the presence of the Spirit enabling them to embrace others and the world in love.

4. The Multiplicity of the Church. The net drew in fish of every kind. The good fish were not all of one kind. In the church it is not external or surface conditions which distinguish the good from the bad. The church encompasses all those who receive Christ and bear fruits of the kingdom regardless of race, ethnicity, nationality, cultural distinctions, economic status, social rank, or gender. The church also includes persons who are at different stages in their growth toward full maturity in Christ. The church does not exclude merely because of differences, but nourishes, encourages, and supports each other in the pursuit of realization of the kingdom among us.

5. The Sea. In Hebrew culture the sea and the desert were generally symbolic of the untamed forces of the world which tend toward chaos. God is the being who brings order out of the chaotic forces of the world. We bring order into the chaotic and untamed urges in our lives when we submit them to the order of God's rule. We also then identify the sources of chaos in the world around us. Secure under the sovereignty of God who is working to order the world, we can face the uncertainties of life and overcome them. Even death loses its fear because we know the order of grace which transcends the world and death.

6. Scribes trained for the kingdom. Jesus was in frequent conflict with the scribes whom he confronted. They were trained in the dead letter of the law. He was angered by the way their sophistry enabled them to rationalize actions which in effect defeated the intention of the law. They failed to recognize the true moving of the spirit of life. One does not have to have all knowledge to be a scribe in the kingdom. A scribe trained for the kingdom does need to experience the realities of life. A scribe needs to do what Peter eventually did. He moved beyond a mere verbal confession of Christ to the experience of the power of the resurrection. The scribe trained for the kingdom needs to love Christ and tend his sheep with the knowledge of the love that seeks and saves as a good shepherd.

Homily Hints

1. Finding the Kingdom. (vv. 44-46) People come to the kingdom in different ways. The way they arrive is not the important issue. That they enter the kingdom is the issue.
    A. Finding by Accident
    B. Finding after Long Searching
    C. Entry is Always by Grace

2. The Supreme Treasure Hunt. (vv. 44-46) Life is a search to discover the meaning God intended for human life.
    A. Knowing the Treasure
    B. Seeking the Treasure
    C. The Cost of the Treasure

3. The Paradox of the Kingdom. (vv. 44-46) The contrasts of the values of the kingdom with the accepted values of the world appear to be upside down. What appears to be giving up some values really results in restoring the fullest values to them.
    A. Giving up Self, Finding Self Fulfilled
    B. Giving up Pleasures, Finding Life More Pleasurable
    C. Giving up Life, Finding Eternal Life

4. The Pearl as a Symbol. (vv. 44-45) The pearl is made from life. It is the result of the action of the oyster to deal with an irritation.

    A. Turning Life's Irritations into Jewels. People have taken adversities and turned them into priceless examples of accomplishments.

    B. Surrounding Evil with Love. Transforming evil with good brings beauty in the midst of ugliness.

    C. Overcoming Handicaps. Handicaps often become challenges to excel rather than causes of defeat.

5. Training for the Kingdom. (v. 52) The person who would be a scribe for the kingdom needs to develop discernment.

    A. Discerning the Old and the New

    B. Discerning the Treasure from Trash

    C. Discerning the Good and the Bad

Contact

Points of Contact

1. The Excitement of a Treasure Hunt. A treasure hunt excites the imagination. How excited we would be if we stumbled onto an unexpected treasure — win the lottery, win the sweepstakes, receive a large inheritance unexpectedly, find gold or oil in our backyard. All these allow people to dream about what they could do with such sudden fortune.

Yet often people who do come into such wealth are not happy because of it. They are hounded by people who want to share in their fortune. They discover relatives they never knew existed! They quickly squander the riches and find the enjoyment of their wealth was transitory. They may end up poorer than they were before they suddenly became rich.

What a contrast to those who discover the treasure of the kingdom. It opens ever new vistas of what life is all about. They find themselves with "relatives," brothers and sisters in the faith who do not demand from them but who support and encourage

86

them. Their lives are further enriched by finding an expanded family of faith.

2. True Riches. Jesus admonished his hearers not to lay up for themselves treasure on earth but treasures in heaven (Matthew 7:14-20). How much anxiety and fear we generate when we have our treasures on earth. We try to find security for such treasures by putting them in safe deposit boxes, by building fences or walls, by installing locks to keep people out, or in other ways seek to protect our treasures. People even become prisoners in their own homes trying to keep their treasures secure.

How different it is when we have treasures in the kingdom of heaven. It is not something to be protected from others. Rather it is a joy to share. It opens life to other people. We do not find ourselves impoverished by sharing our treasure. Instead we find our lives enriched and our treasures enlarged in the process.

3. Ever Seeking and Searching. Life is a process of growth. Persons are goal-oriented beings. They are attracted by hope for something better. The longing for fulfillment is finally realized when persons find themselves in harmony with their Creator. They find the longing satisfied when they realize the purpose for which God intended them to be. In the life of the flesh the possibility of continued growth is lifelong. Even when the physical powers begin to fade and falter, spiritual growth remains a continual search to the end of life in the flesh.

4. Worth the Risk. Both the person who found the treasure in the field and the merchant who found the valuable pearl took risks to obtain something they expected to give them greater value. The persons who commit themselves to the kingdom of heaven take the risk that they will find in living the life of the kingdom, the truth about the meaning and purpose of life. It is the great gamble. It bets that in this world they find joy and satisfaction living in the kingdom as already present. It is also the bet that life continues and finds final fulfillment beyond this world. Still, even if this world is all they gain, is it not worth the risk?

Points to Ponder

1. Where is the Treasure? The diversity of the two treasures raises the issue of whether the treasure of the kingdom is multiple or unitary. Do persons find the riches of the kingdom in personal salvation, in the sense of release from sin and guilt? Do they find the treasure in a transformed motivation that leads to an ethical life which puts aside the temptations to find the meaning of life in the pleasures of the flesh, or in the temptations to spiritual pride? Or is the treasure found in the life of the church, in the fellowship and community that offers acceptance, that inspires to higher living, that supports and comforts in times of weakness, pain, and distress? Or is the treasure found in visioning a whole new world and working to bring it to pass? Or is the treasure wrapped up in all the above?

2. How is the Kingdom Found? The two parables have two different ways to find the kingdom. The first has it found by accident. The man stumbled on it unawares. Do some persons come to the kingdom by accident? Do they stumble on it without seeking and yet become aware of its meaning and significance? In the second parable the merchant searched for the pearl, possibly by extensive travel far and wide. Do persons come to the kingdom by searching the scripture and by seeking the preacher who brings them the word? Is the kingdom found in only one way or are many ways open to find it since the Spirit blows where it wills?

3. The Standard of Judgment. Are we judged by our behaviors which are open and visible to all, or are we judged by our motivation, our inner intention and purposing which are so often hidden from others? Some question is raised about the ethics of the man who found the treasure in the field. He used deception to get it by covering it up and paying less for the field than the treasure was worth. Did Jesus condone his actions or only want to emphasize the final outcome? Was it the behavior or the motivation that Jesus drew upon?

4. Justice at the End. Does the parable of the dragnet with its good and bad fish give hope and assurance that the universe ultimately has a moral structure to it? Can we have faith that while it often appears that crime does pay and the evil is winning, in the final outcome of life and history God brings justice? Is it our task to live the life of faithfulness in trust, patience, and perseverance even when it seems that the evil is winning and the good is being defeated? Is our hope in a just outcome to life and history a reasonable hope? If so, how do we act in light of that hope?

5. Interpreting the Net. Is it proper to use allegory in interpreting the parable of the dragnet? Does the boat represent the church that should be gathering the people in by its evangelizing? Or is the basket the church into which the good is gathered? Will history come to an end when the net is full and the time for the separation of the good and bad fishes has come? Are we to do the separation of the fish or are we to leave it to God's especially appointed agents outside of history?

6. Scribes in the Church. The Presbyterian Church has at times made a distinction between the Teaching Elder and the Ruling Elders. The Ruling Elders are lay persons who govern the local congregation. The Teaching Elder is the pastor. He or she is trained to teach the church proper doctrine. Should the pastor be the "scribe ... trained for the kingdom of heaven," or should that be a separate function in the congregation, or should every Christian be such a scribe?

7. The Old and the New. Jesus did not fit very well the categories of liberal and conservative. He valued the scriptures of his day but he also had the courage and wisdom to reinterpret them. Every person probably is a mixture of liberal and conservative. The conservative wants to preserve the values of the past. The liberal wants to adapt to new understandings and conditions. People in their youth tend to want to make the world over in their own image, and thus are inclined to be liberal. As they age, they want to keep that which they have worked to create. So they become conservative. Does not every person at some point quit being a liberal and become a conservative? What is the proper balance between the old and the new that the Christian scribe should seek?

Illustrative Materials

1. Searching, Yet Accidental. Augustine's spiritual experience is well known. He had tried various routes to achieve fulfillment. He was for a time a Manichean. It did not leave him satisfied. He was led in his search by his pious mother Monica, who prayed for him, and by the preaching of Saint Jerome at Milan, which aroused him to search further. He was puzzled when he, a professor of rhetoric, still did not seem to have the joy in the Christian life as did the relatively unlearned monks in the Nubian desert. Then one day as he paced his walled garden in vexation, he heard the children in the next garden playing a game in which they chanted, "Tolle Lege" — "Take and Read." He picked up the scripture, read Romans 13:13-14, and it happened to him. He was converted and became a leading figure in developing the theology of the early church.

2. Contrasting Ways to the Kingdom. Luther searched in a way similar to Augustine. He tried many ways to achieve a sense of salvation. After being frightened almost to death when caught in a thunderstorm and thrown to the ground by lightning, he vowed to give up his study of law and become a monk. He joined one of the strictest orders, the Augustinians. He almost killed himself in ascetic practices, trying to atone for a sense of guilt. Still he did not find peace in his spiritual life. He was sent to Rome to assist in settling a church dispute. While there he went up the Pilate's stairs on his hands and knees, repeating the Lord's prayer in Latin. But he was repulsed by his pilgrimage instead of being assured of salvation. Then as he prepared lectures on Romans, he came to the verse in Romans 1:17 and similar passages which led him to his central theological principle, that of justification by faith. In that study he received almost accidentally what he had long sought. But he was prepared to receive it by his previous dissatisfactions and longings.

3. Trading for Greater Riches. Millard Fuller was a successful business man. At a relatively young age he had become wealthy. Then he decided that he should give up his business and devote the rest of his life to serving others. He found his new role in starting and leading Habitat for Humanity. He has been successful in providing relatively inexpensive housing for thousands around the world. He seems never to have regretted his decision to give up his wealthy business to give others affordable housing as his particular calling in the kingdom.

4. Unexpected Treasure. In October of 1984 a previously unknown painting by William Merritt Chase called *A View of Prospect Park* was bought at a Denver auction for $500. It was dated about 1885-1886. On December 6, 1984, the painting sold at an auction by Sotheby's for $451,000, the highest amount ever paid at an auction for a Chase painting to that date. It was bought by Alexander Galleries in New York.

The painting was bought so cheaply because it had not been authenticated as by Chase. His name was written on it in green paint, but others who examined it thought he would never have written his name that way. (Reported in *Art News*, 84:19-20, Feb. '85.)

5. Rich but Poor. Robert Polchek won $7.5 million in an Ohio Super Lotto. He quit his $14,000-a-year job. He married his high school sweetheart and built a house on eight acres of land he bought. But friends and strangers hassled him for money. He tried to sell his house, but when people found out he was a lottery winner they wanted him to take a lower price for it. Finally he snapped on January 23, 1994. He set his house on fire after calling the Medina County emergency dispatcher. He was arrested by two officers as he sat watching his house burn. On July 12, 1994, he was convicted of felony aggravated arson. He could face the possibility of being sentenced to 10 to 25 years in prison. At this writing he is more likely to receive a maximum fine of $10,000 and be required to reimburse the volunteer fire department $2,500. Though he receives $300,000 each June from his lottery winning, he is an angry man. Family and friends say it ruined him.

7. Unlimited Forgiveness

Matthew 18:21-35

Then Peter came and said to him, "Lord, if another member of the church sins against me, how often should I forgive? As many as seven times?" [22]Jesus said to him, "Not seven times, but, I tell you, seventy-seven times.

[23]"For this reason the kingdom of heaven may be compared to a king who wished to settle accounts with his slaves. [24]When he began the reckoning, one who owed him ten thousand talents was brought to him; [25]and, as he could not pay, his lord ordered him to be sold, together with his wife and children and all his possessions, and payment to be made. [26]So the slave fell on his knees before him, saying, 'Have patience with me, and I will pay you everything.' [27]And out of pity for him, the lord of that slave released him and forgave him the debt. [28]But that same slave, as he went out, came upon one of his fellow slaves who owed him a hundred denarii; and seizing him by the throat, he said, 'Pay what you owe.' [29]Then his fellow slave fell down and pleaded with him, 'Have patience with me, and I will pay you.' [30]But he refused; then he went and threw him into prison until he would pay the debt. [31]When his fellow slaves saw what had happened, they were greatly distressed, and they went and reported to their lord all that had taken place. [32]Then his lord summoned him and said to him, 'You wicked slave! I forgave you all that debt because you pleaded with me. [33]Should you not have had mercy on your fellow slave,

as I had mercy on you?' [34]And in anger his lord handed him over to be tortured until he would pay his entire debt. [35]So my heavenly Father will also do to every one of you, if you do not forgive your brother or sister from your heart."

The parable uses the analogy of a reverse comparison. On the one hand a huge, almost inconceivable debt is forgiven. The amount of the debt of the first character in the parable is staggering. To the person hearing the parable it would be scarcely possible to imagine a debt so monumental, perhaps as hard as to try to imagine today the size of the national debt in the United States.

The second character has a relatively trivial debt. It is more the size one might run up on a credit card. Such a debt today would hardly bring a person to the court to declare bankruptcy. Most institutions would be ready to try to work out some process for repaying the debt a little at a time rather than have the person go bankrupt.

Such is the scenario which Jesus used to contrast two situations of forgiveness in the parable.

Context

Context of Matthew 18

Chapter 18 contains another block of teaching material inserted by Matthew into the general chronology of the Gospel according to Mark. The chapter is sometimes referred to as the teachings about the church. It follows immediately after Jesus' teaching about how to handle disagreements in the church. That teaching apparently prompted Peter to ask a question about forgiveness and it became the occasion for Jesus to tell the parable of the unforgiving servant.

Context of the Lectionary

The First Lesson. (Exodus 14:19-31) The story is told of the Egyptians following after the Israelites, who were led and protected by the Lord. When the Egyptians entered into the sea in pursuit of the Israelites, Moses let the waters return and engulf the Egyptians. Thus the Israelites were delivered and the mighty works of God were made manifest.

The Second Lesson. (Romans 14:1-12) Paul deals here with the issue of judging. He begins with a plea to recognize the weak in faith and not to use this for an occasion for quarreling over differences. He then proceeds to the problem of the members of the church judging one another. He is concerned about the disruption of the fellowship within the church. The issue is one of self-righteousness over a question about the significance of which day is best for worship. He ends by calling the members of the church to respect each other's convictions, since we all "will be accountable to God." Paul admonishes the readers not to preempt the prerogative of God by presuming which person knows better how to honor God by selecting a particular day to show the honor.

Gospel. (Matthew 18:21-35) The parable tells of the forgiving king and the unforgiving servant. A contrast is made between the king who forgives a great debt and the servant who being forgiven a great debt turns around and refuses to forgive another who owes him a relatively small debt.

Psalm. (Psalm 114) The psalm observes that Israel was liberated from Egypt and made a sanctuary. Even the sea and the mountains responded to this great event. They did so because of the overwhelming presence of God.

Context of related Scriptures

> Genesis 4:24 — The forgiveness of Cain. The mark keeps
>   him from being punished for the murder of Abel.
> Amos 2:6 — The Lord's threefold forgiveness for selling
>   fellow Jews into slavery.
> Amos 8:6 — A warning to those who sell others into slavery.

95

Nehemiah 5:4-5 — The people's cry against the imposition of the king's tax which forces them to sell their children into slavery so they can pay it.

Matthew 5:7 — Mercy returned to the merciful.

Matthew 6:14-15 — The commentary on forgiveness in the Lord's Prayer.

Matthew 14:14 — The compassion of Jesus on the people who were sick.

Matthew 20:34 — The compassion of Jesus for the blind men of Jericho.

Luke 7:41-43 — A somewhat parallel parable about the contrast between two persons with debts of varying magnitude.

Ephesians 4:32 — Paul's call to forgive one another as Christ has forgiven us.

Precis of the Parable

The first part of the parable begins with a king who had a deputy or governor of a district. The amount of income for which the subordinate was accountable to the king was an astounding amount. No indication is given as to why the amount was not available, whether because of the laxness in collecting the taxes or the misuse of the funds in administration of the district. The point is the magnanimous action of the king in overlooking the incompetence or corruption of the official when he pleaded his case.

The pity of the king is contrasted with that of the same official who proceeds to try to collect on a debt another person owed him. The official had the slave thrown into prison until the debt would be paid, probably by other members of his family.

When the king received a report of what the official had done to a fellow slave, he was outraged. He proceeded to have the official suffer the consequences he had tried to evade in the first instance. The analogy of the parable is then applied to how Christians should relate one to another.

Thesis: Gratitude for divine forgiveness should lead to readiness to reciprocate to others.

Theme: Failure to forgive has dire consequences.

Key Words of the Parable

1. "Seven Times." (v. 21) Seven was a number that had the quality of completeness or perfection. Peter no doubt thought he was proposing considerable generosity when he asked if forgiving seven times was enough. Most people would think that forgiving seven times was more than sufficient latitude to offer anyone.

2. "Seventy-seven times." (v. 22) Jesus raises the amount from seven to a number that would be hard to keep track of. Some manuscripts even make the exaggeration more extreme by saying seventy-times seven, or a total of 490 times, ten times more than the square of the number Peter suggests.

3. "A King." (v. 23) In rabbinical writing a king was often a protagonist and served as a symbol for God.

4. "Ten Thousand Talents." (v. 24) A worker would have to work 15 years to earn a talent, according to some authorities. Others propose it would be the equivalent of $1000. Thus ten thousand talents would be worth $10,000,000. For that period it was about as large an amount as could be imagined.

5. "Him to be sold, with ... wife, ... children." (v. 25) Selling people into slavery, either from greed or to pay a debt, sometimes occurred, but was condemned by the prophets. (See Amos 2:6, 8:6; Nehemiah 5:4-5.) The sale of wife and children was probably as much for punishment as for payment of the debt.

6. "The Debt." (v. 27) The amount was probably a loan though some suggest it may have been taxes collected and owed to the king by a district governor.

7. "A Hundred Denarii." (v. 28) A denarius in a subsistence economy that did not depend heavily on cash but rather engaged more often in barter was a typical wage for a day's work. One hundred denarii is estimated to be about $20.

8. "Handed him over to be tortured." (v. 34) Torture was often used either to extract a confession or to force a payment of a debt. Given the magnitude of the debt in this case, it was probably understood as a punishment deserved, both for the debt owed and for his mistreatment of his fellow servant.

9. "Pay his entire debt." (v. 34) The sentence was tantamount to life imprisonment since he would likely not be able to pay such a huge debt, especially if in prison where he would be unable to acquire any wealth.

10. "From your heart." (v. 35) The forgiveness had to be more than a simple "I'm sorry." It had to be a sincere change of attitude toward the one who had done the wrong.

Contemplation

Insights

1. Unlimited forgiveness. It has been proposed that the biblical understanding of retaliation and forgiveness developed progressively. In the original impulse toward wrongdoing, retaliation was unlimited. In the cases of the violation by Achan at Ai, the people not only stoned him, but also his sons and daughters and his oxen, donkeys, and sheep (Joshua 7). And the same was also done to the inhabitants of Ai when they were conquered (Joshua 8). In the latter case they practiced ethnic cleansing! Later "limited retaliation" became the norm in the principle of equality — "an eye for an eye, and a tooth for a tooth" (Matthew 5:38). Peter in verse 21 was for "limited forgiveness" within the church when he proposed forgiving seven times. Jesus instead called for "unlimited forgiveness." Seven times 70, or 70 times 70, would be understood as infinite forgiveness.

2. Reciprocal Action. In the Lord's Prayer Jesus taught his disciples to pray "and forgive us our debts, as we also have forgiven our debtors" (Matthew 6:12). The heart of the parable is found in verse 35 where the heavenly Father treats everyone as they have genuinely acted toward brothers and sisters. In physics a basic law states that for every action there is an equal but opposite reaction. This parable proposes a different spiritual law: For every action toward a brother or sister, an equal action occurs. Lack of forgiveness equals lack of forgiveness, but forgiveness equals forgiveness.

3. God's Grace is Unlimited. No matter how great our debt, God's mercy and pity is sufficient to cover it. When we present ourselves before God with readiness to accept his grace, we can be assured that it is offered. No matter how grievous our past debt we can approach the Lord without fear that God seeks our destruction. Rather God constantly seeks our redemption.

4. The Greater and the Lesser. The human debt before God is larger than any person can repay. Total obedience to the will of God is demanded. People assert their will over against God, incurring an insurmountable debt had they been dealing with a bookkeeping Lord. The debt which any other person might owe us for the wrong done to us has to be trivial compared to our debt in God's sight. If God can forgive us so great a debt, we should be prepared to forgive the much smaller debt which we might feel is due us.

5. Breaking the Cycle of Revenge. Gandhi said that if people practice an eye for an eye and a tooth for a tooth, we will soon live in a society of the blind and toothless. The legendary feud of the Hatfields and the McCoys continued a cycle of revenge from generation to generation, threatening to wipe out both clans. The massacres in Bosnia and Rwanda demonstrate the human disasters that flow from accumulations of wrongs from generations past. The cycle of revenge is broken when persons realize God's forgiveness and break the cycle of revenge by being prepared to offer forgiveness themselves. But the forgiveness has to be genuine, which means offering more than a formal expression of it. It means accepting the other party as brothers and sisters. Should the Christian response not be ethnic cleansing, but the obliteration of ethnic differences by accepting others as one in Christ? Should this be done, not because they deserve it or because they have accepted Christ, but because that is what God is offering them and inviting them to become? Should we not be God's agents at the point where we can offer them forgiveness?

Homily Hints

1. The Dynamics of Forgiveness. (vv. 18-35)
A. The Recognition of Our Debt. The first step is to recognize our need for forgiveness.
B. The Acceptance of Forgiveness. We need to accept forgiveness and forgive ourselves.
C. The Response to Forgiveness. Forgiveness makes us compassionate and merciful to others who need our forgiveness if our forgiveness is to be completed.

2. Seventy Times Seven [or Seventy]. (vv. 21-22) A church leader once said in response to the generosity of a business man, "I am glad to know such a person who understands spiritual mathematics."
A. Human Mathematics. Balance sheets have to total up assets and liabilities, income and expenses so that they balance each other. Too often human relationships operate on such bookkeeping of accounts.
B. Spiritual Mathematics. Spiritual accounting responds to human need rather than to balance sheets.
C. A New Equation. In spiritual equations we do not have to balance both sides of an equation. We have to balance the greater of God with the lesser of human reactions.

3. Blessed are the Merciful. (v. 33) The merciful are happy because they learn that they too receive mercy.

    A. Compassion. We enter into the condition of others to the extent that we understand our own condition.

    B. Reversing Normal Psychology. People generally justify their own actions by external causes which are not their fault but attribute to others blame for their similar actions as intentional. Jesus calls us to accept responsibility for our actions but to understand other's actions compassionately.

    C. Enlarging Self. By entering into the experiences of others and suffering with them even in their failures, we enlarge ourselves.

4. Face to Face Answers. (v. 35) The reciprocal nature of human interaction is asserted in this proverb (see Proverbs 27:19).

    A. We See Ourselves in Others. The tendency is to expect of others the worst actions we find in ourselves.

    B. Rising Above Ourselves. Instead of looking at others as a mirror of ourselves, we need to look at others as God sees them.

    C. Seeing Ourselves in God's Action. We become greater by looking at the greatest and thereby seeing our fullest possibilities.

5. Demythologizing Revenge and Forgiveness. (vv. 22, 34-35) Look at false understandings of revenge and forgiveness. Address some of the false answers people give to them.

    A. Is Revenge Sweet?

    B. Is Forgiveness Only a Duty?

    C. Is Forgiveness a Sign of Weakness?

Contact

Points of Contact or to Ponder

1. Restoring Relationships. Relationships are broken

when a person does wrong to another or one feels wronged by another. The act sets up a barrier between the persons. Only forgiveness, whether in some formal act, such as an apology or request for forgiveness, or in acted out forgiveness, removes the barrier and restores the relationship. In most instances in life no formal act of forgiveness takes place. The forgiveness takes place implicitly in people's acceptance of each other. Nevertheless, it is dangerous to assume that we are forgiven without a formal acknowledgement by both parties. Otherwise the situation may fester and continue to disrupt the relationship.

2. Guilt: True or False. One of the problems people face is to distinguish between real guilt and a false sense of guilt. Two aspects of a false sense of guilt may need to be considered. Sometimes in the course of life and our human interdependence we may hurt another person when we are not really guilty. An example might be when we have an auto accident due to a mechanical failure and someone else is injured or killed. If we have been responsible in maintaining a safe vehicle and in driving in a manner regarded as safe, we are not blameworthy for the accident. Still we may feel guilty. We need to distinguish between remorse and guilt. In remorse we may be sorry that the ill happened, but we are not guilty and in need of forgiveness. Nevertheless, we may face a problem because other persons may feel we are blameworthy. People may need to seek forgiveness, not because of real guilt, but because of perceived guilt on the part of others. In guilt we are to blame for what happened and need forgiveness.

3. Intended and Unintended. Intention or the perception of intention adds to the feeling of being wronged by another person. How often are we much more ready to forgive or excuse an act that is unintended. If we are riding a crowded bus and the jerking of the vehicle causes us to bump another person, it is easily excused. If, however, we intentionally push a person aside so we can get through the crowded bus, the action is seen as intentional. Persons are then more likely to be offended and less likely to accept our "I'm sorry" even though the bump may be less than the one described earlier.

4. Guilt Unaware. We may have a problem when we are unaware of a wrong we have done to another. We all probably have what are called ethical blind spots. What we have considered to be acceptable behavior because of our family, social, or cultural customs may offend someone with a different background. We are much more aware today than we were years ago of how language may reflect offensive attitudes that harm other people. Still we may use language that demeans or insults others when we are unaware that it does so. What obligation does the person who is offended or insulted have to raise our consciousness and enable us to be forgiven?

5. The Privilege of Forgiving. The parable infers that we have the privilege to be agents of forgiveness. If God has forgiven us so much of our past guilt, in gratitude we should become agents of God's mercy and compassion. It is a great privilege and opportunity to show the nature of God by forgiving as we have experienced forgiveness. Indeed, have we really known God's forgiveness of us unless we likewise take the opportunity to forgive others?

6. Forgiving Institutions. How do you forgive institutions? Church institutions as much as others often need to be forgiven. Many churches have split over disputes that occurred in the past. The occasions or reasons for the disputes or mistakes made may be years in the past and no longer in the memory of present members. Still the broken relations continue. Persons carry grudges against institutional grievances long into the future. How do we deal with the need for institutions, both sacred and secular, to be forgiven, especially if the parties to the cause of the grievance are long gone and present members have no sense of personal guilt?

7. Conditions for Forgiveness. Does forgiveness require certain conditions for it to be fulfilled? Forgiveness has two sides: the person needing forgiveness and the person offering forgiveness. Can we really forgive another unless the other person repents of the action and regrets the act sufficiently not to want to do it again? Sometimes persons ask for forgiveness in advance. How can they be forgiven if they intend to continue doing the act? Does forgiveness not sanction continuation of the behavior that is unacceptable? Can we really forgive another unless we ourselves have experienced it from another and accepted it from ourselves? Jesus admonished Peter to forgive seven (or 70) times seven. Should battered wives and children continue to accept the abuse of husbands and fathers? Is the offer of forgiveness conditional on a change of behavior?

Illustrative Materials

1. Getting Back What We Give. A story is told of a family moving to a new town. They stopped near the town to talk to a farmer working in a field. They asked him what the people were like in the town. He in turn asked them how they liked the town they had left. They said that the people were terrible. They were leaving because they did not like the town and were looking for a better place. The farmer told them they should look for another town since they would find the people in his town just the same.

A while later another family came along and stopped to talk to the same farmer. They asked what the people were like in his town. Again he asked how they found the town they left. They said that the people were wonderful. They hated to leave, but they found it necessary to do so. He told them they would find the people in his town the same way and they would probably be glad to live there.

2. A Forgiving Act. During a time of civil unrest in Russia a group of men came at night and began removing the roof of a house that belonged to a family which did not support them. Hearing the commotion, the man of the house looked out and saw what they were doing. He went out and said they must be tired from their work and invited them in for some hot coffee and bread. They came and ate. Then sheepishly they returned to their work, only this time they put the tiles back on the roof and left without further animosity toward the family.

3. An Unforgiving Society. During the hostage crisis in Iran a group of Americans visited in an attempt to open a dialogue of reconciliation. In the process they asked the students who were holding the hostages what the Shah could do to be forgiven. Could he return his riches to the country? Could he repent of the evils he had done? The students replied that he could do nothing to be forgiven. He had to pay his debt to the society, which obviously meant that he had to be tried and executed. Some members of the American party felt that was a difference between their understanding of religion and a Christian approach which would offer forgiveness upon repentance and an attempt to make restitution.

4. Forgiveness and Illness. A pastoral counselor told of a woman who had a severe illness. The doctors thought her illness was terminal and that they could do nothing to heal her. She came from a tradition which believed in anointing by oil for sickness (as found in James 5:14). She requested that the elders of the church do that. They came but before they anointed her they inquired about her spiritual condition. They discovered that she was filled with bitterness about life and certain people's actions toward her. They first had her confess her bitterness and resentment of others. Then they did the anointing as a symbol of her forgiveness. She had a quick and amazing recovery. The doctors could not understand how she was healed even though some scar tissue was still evidence of the previous illness.

5. A Cycle of War. After World War I heavy reparations were demanded of Germany. As a consequence the German economy suffered and the people felt that they were treated unjustly. Many historians feel that the high demands of vengeance wreaked on Germany laid the seeds for World War II. After World War II no great reparations were demanded. Instead the Marshall Plan helped western Europe as a whole to recover. Germany responded by becoming one of the strongest allies of the western powers which had defeated it. The cycle of war was stopped.

6. Acted Forgiveness. A group of families were engaged

in a housing project where they worked cooperatively. Some of the young men were assigned to haul some materials from a coal mining dump to build the roads. To get to the materials they had to go almost a mile out of the way around a small creek. When they had the dump truck loaded it was close to time for lunch. The driver decided that he would just go through the small creek since it only had about a half foot of water in it. Midway through the truck got stuck. The young men tried to get it out. They even unloaded the truck and tried shoveling the materials under the wheels, but with the water the wheels just spun the materials out again. By that time the truck was resting on its differential. Finally one of the men walked about three miles to get the Quaker project manager to come with the tractor and pull the truck out. He came and never said a word of anger or reprimand. After the truck was free and he had returned to the project, the driver of the truck exclaimed, "If he had only bawled us out, I could feel better about what we did!" The young men never tried the shortcut again.

7. A Family Feud in a Congregation. Two families had a bitter dispute. For years afterward they would never speak to one another even though two of the participants were brother and sister. It became an unwritten rule in the church that you could never put the parents of these two families on the same committee or board. It not only poisoned the relationships between the two families, but infected the church. It was a situation which no one talked about anymore but simply accepted as the way things were in the congregation.

8. Service And Reward

Matthew 20:1-16

"*For The kingdom of heaven is like a landowner who went out early in the morning to hire laborers for his vineyard. [2]After agreeing with the laborers for the usual daily wage, he sent them into his vineyard. [3]When he went out about nine o'clock, he saw others standing idle in the marketplace; [4]and he said to them, 'You also go into the vineyard, and I will pay you whatever is right.' So they went. [5]When he went out again about noon and three o'clock, he did the same. [6]And about five o'clock he went out and found others standing around; and he said to them, 'Why are you standing here idle all day?' [7]They said to him, 'Because no one has hired us.' He said to them, 'You also go into the vineyard.' [8]When evening came, the owner of the vineyard said to his manager, 'Call the laborers and give them their pay, beginning with the last and then going to the first.' [9]When those hired about five o'clock came, each of them received the usual daily wage. [10]Now when the first came, they thought they would receive more; but each of them also received the usual daily wage. [11]And when they received it, they grumbled against the landowner, [12]saying, 'These last worked only one hour, and you have made them equal to us who have borne the burden of the day and the scorching heat.' [13]But he replied to one of them, 'Friend, I am doing you no wrong; did you not agree with me for the usual daily wage? [14]Take what belongs to you, and go; I choose to give to this last the same as I give*

107

to you. ¹⁵Am I not allowed to do what I choose with what belongs to me? Or are you envious because I am generous?' ¹⁶So the last will be first, and the first will be last."

Social status may be determined by many factors. Some of these may be given by birth, genetics, or for reasons other than the achievement of the person. These include such things as color of skin and eyes, kind of hair, height, body build, gender, national origin, family's social position, inherited wealth, and age.

Other factors may be determined by achievements through a person's efforts. These include such factors as level of education, employment, development of skills, hard work, wise investment, or initiatives taken.

People who have sought to improve their social and economic status by what they have achieved may resent the higher status of others who were given their status by the accident of birth or nationality or family connections. It would appear to them that life has not been fair.

The parable of the laborers who worked longer than others in the vineyard seems to suggest an unfairness in the rewards in the kingdom of heaven. The actions of Jesus do suggest that he was not ready to judge persons by normal standards of determining social status. The parable proposes a different basis for receiving salvation than the way in which persons are generally rewarded by society.

Context

Context of the Gospels

Matthew has set the parable that is unique to his gospel in the context of events which both Mark and Luke have. The encounter with the rich young ruler (Matthew 19:16-30, Mark 10:17-31, Luke 18:18-30) leads the disciples to raise questions about whether they will be rewarded for the sacrifices they have made. Matthew uses that as the specific occasion for Jesus' telling of the parable.

The parable is also in the context of two other events when people tried to exclude other persons from Jesus' attention. The first precedes the location of the parable by Matthew (Matthew 19:13-15, Mark 10:13-16, Luke 18:15-17). It is the attempt of the disciples to protect Jesus' time by excluding the children. Jesus reprimands the disciples for doing so and proceeds to bless the children and then uses them as an example of those who will receive the kingdom of heaven. The children do not receive the blessing from Jesus for what they have done but just for who they are and because of his graciousness.

The second is the healing of two blind men in Jericho whom the crowd tried to exclude by admonishing them to be quiet. (Matthew 20:19-34; only one blind person in Mark and Luke: Mark 10:46-52, Luke 18:35-43.) The blind man, once healed, immediately becomes a follower of Jesus out of gratitude for the blessing of sight that he received.

The context also includes the request of the mother of James and John to seek a privileged position in the kingdom. (It is also found in Mark 10:35-45, but not in Luke.) Jesus used the question to assert that greatness in the kingdom is by servanthood. He also asks them if they are willing to face the same difficulties which Jesus anticipated for himself and his followers.

Context of Matthew

The parable is bracketed by two variations of the statement, "But many who are first will be last, and the last will be first" (Matthew 19:30), and the inversion of it, "So the last will be first, and the first will be last" (Matthew 20:16). According to Matthew Jesus continues to use the various events to communicate his vision of what the kingdom of heaven is like and how it differs from current common conceptions of it. Immediately preceding the parable when Jesus accepts the children and blesses them, he uses them as a model as to how the kingdom is granted by grace where other persons would exclude them. Then in the encounter with the rich young man, he indicates that it is almost impossible for anyone to be worthy of the kingdom on the basis of his or her actions.

The First Lesson. (Exodus 16:2-15) The people in the desert complain against Moses and Aaron for bringing them out into the wilderness where they fear they will starve. God then assures Moses that he will provide bread daily for them to eat. They will have enough for daily food except on the sixth day they will have twice as much as needed so they can observe the Sabbath of rest. Then the people will know the glory of the Lord who can provide for their needs. They will have no further reason for complaining against the leaders whom the Lord has appointed.

The Second Lesson. (Philippians 1:21-30) Paul affirms his own life to be in accordance with his understanding of the kingdom of heaven. He desires to depart and realize the full presence of Christ and his kingdom. But he also understands that his mission is to have those whom he brought into the church have the full knowledge of the meaning of the gospel which had transformed his life. This knowledge will not be for the destruction of their opponents but for salvation for the Philippians. They can be assured of their salvation because they are now having the same struggles which Paul had.

Gospel. (Matthew 20:1-16) The parable revolves about the equal rewards given to workers in the vineyard for unequal amounts of labor.

Psalm. (Psalm 105:1-6, 37-45) The psalmist calls the people to give thanks. They are to remember the miracles which the Lord has done in the past. The latter verses recount the experience of the Israelites being brought out of Egypt with riches and then reminds them of the way in which the Lord provided for the Israelites in the desert as is told in the passage in the first lesson for today. The gratitude for the memory of God's provisions should lead them to be obedient to God's statutes and laws. In such manner they will praise the glory of the Lord.

Leviticus 19:l3 — The law against oppressing or robbing neighbors. Do not keep a hired servant's wages overnight.

Deuteronomy 24:15 — The need to pay laborers before sunset.

Psalm 24:1 — The divine ownership of the earth.

Jeremiah 12:10 — Shepherds ruin the vineyard.

Malachi 3:5 — Judgment against those who defraud by withholding wages.

Mark 7:22 — Jesus' teaching about the sins of the heart, including covetousness and envy.

Luke 3:14 — John the Baptist tells soldiers to be content with their wages.

Philippians 4:11 — Paul's contention that "In whatever state I am, to be content."

Colossians 4:1— Paul's admonition to masters to treat their slaves fairly.

James 5:4 — A condemnation of those who don't pay persons who mow the field.

Content

Content of the Pericope

Jesus tells a parable about a landowner who, apparently at the peak of the harvest season, hired temporary workers five times during the day at about three hour intervals. He negotiates with the first workers to pay them the normal wage for a day. With the other workers he only agrees to pay them what is right.

At the end of the day the landowner instructs his manager to pay each of the workers the normal daily wage. The workers who were hired first and worked for 12 hours expected to be paid more, especially more than those who only worked one hour. When they got the same amount as the others, they complained about its unfairness.

The landowner reminds them that they got what they had

agreed to as a fair wage. He then poses rhetorical questions as to his right to choose to do as he pleased with what he owned and whether they resented that he was a generous person.

The point of the parable is given at the end: "So the last will be first and the first last." The parable is given in response to the query from the disciples as to whether they would be rewarded for their faithfulness in following Jesus and enduring the hardships and sacrifices of such life.

Thesis: Salvation is not earned by efforts but is given by grace according to a person's need.

Theme: Kingdom rewards are given generously to those who enter it.

Key Words in the Parable

1. "Landowner." (v. 1) God is the sovereign who owns the earth. People are called to be laborers for God.

2. "Laborer." (v. 1) Those who enter the kingdom have a task to do. To care for a vineyard requires a lot of tedious hand labor, both in pruning the vines at the beginning of the growing season and at harvest time.

3. "Vineyard." (v. 1) A vineyard is often used as an image for God's kingdom.

4. "Early." (v.1) The day started at sunrise, which was normally 6 a.m. It was designated as the first hour in their system of reckoning.

5. "Usual Daily Wage." (v. 2) A denarius was usually considered a daily wage. An oral agreement was binding under the law at that time.

6. "Standing Idle." (v. 3) Literally it says they were

"hanging about." Day laborers would assemble in the marketplace of a town or village. Employers who needed temporary help would go there and select the number they needed. The marketplace served as the employment office in that culture. If men were not hired, they would linger there with nothing to do.

7. "Pay you whatever is right." (v. 4) The men were in no position to bargain. Earning anything was probably better for them than spending the day idle. They had to rely on the fairness of the employer.

8. "About Five O'Clock." (v. 6) The landowner went very late in the day, with only about an hour of time left. No explanation is given as to why these men were still in the marketplace and had not been hired earlier. Presumably the landowner was anxious to get the grapes harvested before the rains came and spoiled them.

9. "No One has Hired Us." (v. 7) Some reproach is implied in the question about why they were still there. The men became defensive. During the harvest season plenty of work should be available for anyone who was willing to work.

10. "Each of Them Received the Usual Daily Wage." (v. 9) The owner knew that the men had to provide for families. They needed the usual wage or their families would go hungry.

11. "Friend." (v. 13) Is the term an implied reproach? It was the same address Jesus used with Judas when betrayed in the Garden of Gethsemane (Matthew 26:50). Jesus also addresses his disciples in a similar fashion (See John 15:15).

12. "I Choose." (v. 14) It was the prerogative of the owner to use his possessions as he wished. As long as he paid a fair wage to the workers who labored all day they had no reason to complain even though the inequity between their effort and the reward seemed unfair compared to the other workers.

13. "Are You Envious?" (v. 15) Literally the expression is "Is your eye evil?"

Contemplation

Insights

1. What is Justice? The word justice is slippery. It can have different meanings to different people or in different circumstances. One standard, and probably the most frequent one, is that of equality. Everyone should be treated equally. A frequent slogan in labor-management negotiation which embodies this concept of justice is "Equal pay for equal work."

Another standard has a similar basis but is dependent on merit. You should get what you deserve. This principle is found in "piece work" as opposed to an hourly or daily wage. It is assumed that if people are more productive, they deserve more pay. It is generally assumed that a person with more education and higher skills deserves more reward. Thus a doctor who invests years in getting an education and honing skills deserves more per hour than someone who goes to work right out of high school.

A third standard is based on need. The Marxist principle, "From each according to ability; to each according to need," comes out of Karl Marx's Judeo-Christian background (See Acts 2:45). The owner in the parable seems to have combined a principle of equality (all received equal pay) with a sense of need (generosity to those who only worked at the end of the day.) The workers who labored all day thought the pay was unjust on the basis of merit, what they deserved.

It is generally agreed that Jesus is not proposing a general economic principle in this parable, but emphasizing the generosity of God in rewarding those who enter the kingdom, regardless of when in life they respond to God's call.

2. Service and Reward. A distinction sometimes is made between work and play. It is the difference between extrinsic and intrinsic rewards. It is work when persons have to be paid for efforts beyond what they get in terms of satisfaction from the activity itself. Persons have to have a monetary reward for engaging in certain activities or they would not do it.

Play is when people just enjoy doing what they are doing, regardless of whether they get any reward otherwise. The effort expended is not the measure of whether it is work. Enjoyment in doing something is its own reward in play.

The parable suggests that service in the kingdom is more of the nature of play. It has its reward in doing the right thing, not because of the amount of extrinsic reward. Nevertheless, God is good and generous and the rewards received may be well beyond our deserving in a strictly egalitarian sense.

3. Working in the Lord's Vineyard. The English language has no equivalent play on words to that of the German for the expression "The kingdom is both *Gabe* and *Aufgabe*." *Gabe* is the German word for *gift* and *Aufgabe* is the word for a *task*. The kingdom is both a gift and a task.

Some confusion exists between the giving of salvation by grace, and the doing of kingdom work as a task. Persons do not receive the kingdom because they deserve it. It is offered to all by the grace of God. As Lord he is a good and generous giver.

However, once the gift is received, it is a call to a life of obedience to God's will. As such it is a task that is more a response of gratitude for the privilege of being in the kingdom than as the reward that is offered at the end of life.

4. The Lord is Sovereign. What we receive from the earth is not simply something we have a right to have. We have the earth in trust as co-creators with God in bringing God's will to complete fulfillment. With God as sovereign Lord, we are to work in the vineyard and not to destroy it. The earth is created with amazing recuperative powers. Nevertheless it has limits and the resources are finite.

The earth is intended to provide us with our daily needs. Our needs should be met with consideration for the needs of others and of those to come in later generations. We should use the resources to meet our needs with care, and not with envy of those who acquire in excess of their daily needs.

5. The Inversion of Values. Matthew frames the parable with the warning that the first will be last and the last will be first. So often the kingdom values are the opposite of worldly values.

The events recorded just prior to the parable led Jesus to contrast the kingdom with conventional wisdom. The first incident was the blessing of the children. They model the kingdom in their innocence and directness. They are not engaged in the intrigue and deception so often characterized by adults. They are themselves and do not attempt to mislead others as to who they are in order to manipulate and gain advantage over others.

The second incident was the encounter with the "poor" rich man. He wanted a quick and easy way to salvation. He had no real sense of his need to change. He manifested a certain smugness in his good behavior. He saw nothing in his life that would call for a radical transformation. He was possessed by his possessions. So he missed the opportunity to participate with the followers of Jesus in the joy of sharing in the work of the kingdom.

As the disciples looked at the young man and compared his lot in life with theirs, they may have had a question about whose life was better. Jesus does not think that many possessions make a person rich. Rather it is the commitment to the kingdom and its values that gives true and enduring meaning to life.

Homily Hints

1. The Good Landowner. (vv. 1-15) The actions of the landowner reveal Jesus' understanding of the nature of God.
> A. The Generous God. God provides for daily needs for those who labor in the kingdom. His grace is not conditioned on what we deserve. It is dependent on our real needs.
> B. The Seeking God. The owner returned again and again to the market place to see if any were still idle. He offered all a place to work in the vineyard, even those whom others had rejected.

C. The Sovereign God. The owner had the right to choose how the goods were to be distributed. The standards for reward were not always according to conventional wisdom. God's awareness of need is larger than the human tendency to be centered in one's own needs or desires, and not to be equally concerned with the needs of others.

2. The Right Side Up Kingdom. (v. 16)
A. The False Values Turned Around. God corrects false values when people get obsessed with who is number one.
B. Supplying Daily Needs. Jesus understood that the daily needs of people have to be met. People are not just spiritual beings. They have physical needs as well. Physical needs once met should serve the spirit and not become ends in themselves.
C. Fulfilling Human Potential. Care needs to be taken that fulfilling human potential is not confounded with thinking that people are the sole source of salvation. Some people seem to be so concerned about a philosophy of humanism that they end up appearing to be anti-human. Jesus always loved people and was incensed when they were prevented from realizing their full and true humanity.

3. Invidious Comparisons. (v. 12)
A. Corrosive Envy. Comparison of a person's gifts with others can disrupt relationships. Persons' self-esteem can be damaged if they look at the gifts others have instead of accepting and using the gifts they have.
B. Jealous of Position. Often church fights arise because people want positions of power. They resent others who have positions they want to have so as to control the institutions and others.
C. Measured by Christ. The antidote to corrosive envy is to look at oneself in comparison with Christ and not

with other people. The goal is to emulate the servanthood and cross bearing of Christ, not to compare oneself to other people.

4. What Time is It? (vv. 1-15)
A. Early Arrivals. The people who are privileged to enter the church early have a lifetime to enjoy labor in the kingdom.
B. Late Arrivals. People who have had long membership in the church may envy those who enter late and their freshness and enthusiasm. The late arrivals may seem to surpass or even displace the long-term members of the church. It is a danger that may affect the harmony of the church.
C. Never Too Late. God continues to seek those who are outside the kingdom. Despite a long life outside the kingdom, it is never too late to be accepted. Entrance into the church as representative of the kingdom is not just for the young.

5. Kingdom Work. (vv. 1-15)
A. The Scope of Service. It is not just those who are engaged in full-time service, such as the pastor or the director of Christian education, who serve the kingdom.
B. Voluntary Service. Persons may find their service in the kingdom does not have to be paid because their daily needs may be met otherwise. They find their reward entirely intrinsic and do not need extrinsic rewards.
C. Lay Service. Emphasis can be given to the values of lay activity in the Church. Ordained ministers are not set apart because they are more valued but because they have different functions.

6. When is Justice Done? Examine the different standards of justice and their implications for Christian behavior.
A. Equality of Worth
B. Our Just Desserts
C. Love Fulfills Justice

Contact

1. Birthright or Convinced. The Society of Friends (Quakers) make a distinction between birthright Friends and convinced Friends. Those who are birthright Friends were born and raised in a family that was a long-time member of a Friends Meeting. Convinced Friends are those who at some stage in their life became a member by their own choice, even though having no background in the Society. While other religious groups may not have the same terms, jealousy may arise when new members (convinced) receive more attention and seem to be rewarded with positions of prominence and influence.

2. Who Do You Follow? Someone has suggested that with a change of pastor a congregation may actually have two or more sub-congregations in the same church. One congregation may feel their loyalty remains with the previous pastor. Another group may identify with the new pastor. Still others may feel they belong to some earlier beloved pastor. The issue is not to which pastor the congregation owes loyalty. It is rather a question of all giving loyalty to Christ and following him. Otherwise envy and jealousy may leave a congregation divided and struggling over who is rewarded with power in decision making. Those holding loyalty to early pastors may eventually leave the church.

3. A Gap Between Professionals and the Laity. Many churches have moved increasingly to professional leadership. Earlier the church may have only paid the pastor. Now they may have a multiple professional staff, including associate or assistant pastors, directors of Christian education, youth ministers and choir director(s). The church may even pay members of the choir and Sunday school teachers. Compensating persons for their professional service has New Testament support. Problems may arise, however, when members resent being asked to undertake tasks in the church for which others are paid. They may also come to feel that the church really is the professionals and that the laity has no role to play in it.

4. Joy in Service. Happy is the person whose work is play. Members of the church should find joy in their ministering to others. Any extra reward is just a bonus. People should find satisfaction in having opportunity both in serving others in the church and through the church reaching out to serve others. Unhappy is the person who has not learned the joy of service.

Points to Ponder

1. The Pharisees or the Disciples. It is not quite clear who the persons are in the parable who were hired to work at different times during the day. Was it the Pharisees who had sought all their lives to be faithful to God and now envied Jesus and his disciples? Was it the disciples who were with Jesus from the beginning of his public ministry and who were envious of a young man such as the one who asked Jesus what he had to do to be saved? Who are the people today who are like the workers who labored 12 hours and grumbled at the latecomers who received a full day's wage?

2. Retributive Justice. A standard of justice which was not discussed earlier is what is called retributive justice. It is embodied in such phrases as "giving the criminal what he deserves" and "paying a debt to society." It is a reverse side of merit as the standard for justice. The question arises as to whether vengeance is only the prerogative of God. Is a generous and good God only able to mete out justice fairly according to need, just as the parable suggests that reward is according to need and not according to merit on the basis of how much or how long someone has served? What does this parable have to say about the Christian attitude toward criminals, especially those who show repentance and respond to Christ's call?

1. Who is "Church"? A congregation was located in a college town. Most of the residents of the town were of a particular ethnic group. Many of the faculty members at the college joined the church. On one occasion all the delegates to a district conference were members who had come to the church after becoming affiliated with the college. One older member of the congregation complained, "Why don't they appoint some members of 'the church'?" meaning some of the long-term ethnic members of the congregation.

2. Equal and Distributive Justice. During the Depression a family with four children sometimes had one orange for lunch. To assure equitable distribution of the orange the oldest child would cut the orange and then proceeding from the youngest to the oldest the four children chose a quarter section. This assured that the orange would be divided in equal parts since it was presumed that if they were not equal in size, the one who did the cutting would get the smallest portion. She would not want that to happen.

On Sunday the family would have a roast or some other meat. If the pieces were of unequal size, the largest piece always went to the father since he was the wage owner and needed energy for the hard work he did. Need and not equality was the measure of what was fair in that instance.

3. Deathbed Baptism. The emperor Constantine delayed becoming a Christian as long as he could for fear that what he did might prevent him from receiving eternal life. Only when he was on his deathbed did he finally consent to be baptized, so late that he could not do anything to jeopardize his salvation.

4. Give Him a Penny. Pythagoras was a Greek mathematician. He was teaching a group of young people how to do mathematics. One of the students asked him what good this knowledge was going to do for him. Pythagoras told one of his servants to give the student a penny so he would get something out of the study!

5. Status Envy. A group traveled through the South during the time when the nation was becoming aware of racism and civil rights. They talked with some workers in a factory about the need for equality among the races. One of the workers protested, "But if the Negroes are equal with us, no one will be below us!"

6. Seeking Rewards. It is reported that a woman in the Middle Ages went about with a torch and a bucket of water. She wanted to burn heaven and put out the fires of hell so that people would love God for himself alone.

9. Two Sons

Matthew 21:23-32

When he entered the temple, the chief priests and the elders of the people came to him as he was teaching and said, "By what authority are you doing these things, and who gave you this authority?" [24]Jesus said to them, "I will also ask you one question; if you tell me the answer, then I will also tell you by what authority I do these things. [25]Did the baptism of John come from heaven, or was it of human origin?" And they argued with one another, "If we say, 'From heaven,' he will say to us, 'Why then did you not believe him?' [26]But if we say, 'Of human origin,' we are afraid of the crowd; for all regard John as a prophet." [27]So they answered Jesus, "We do not know." And he said to them, "Neither will I tell you by what authority I am doing these things.

[28] "What do you think? A man had two sons; he went to the first and said, 'Son, go and work in the vineyard today.' [29]He answered, 'I will not' ; but later he changed his mind and went. [30]The father went to the second and said the same; and he answered, 'I go, sir' ; but he did not go. [31]Which of the two did the will of his father?" They said, "The first." Jesus said to them, "Truly, I tell you, the tax collectors and the prostitutes are going into the kingdom of God ahead of you. [32]For John came to you in the way of righteousness and you did not believe him, but the tax collectors and the prostitutes believed him; and even after you saw it, you did not change your minds and believe him."

In the current vernacular people speak of those who "talk the talk" in contrast to those who "walk the walk." Those who "talk the talk" are persons who recognize a problem and analyze the situation. They may rant and rave about the difficulties and the need for change. They make accusations against those whom they believe to be responsible for the situation. But they do not move to action to do anything about it nor do they assume responsibility themselves for the existence of the problem when they may be somewhat responsible for it.

Persons who "walk the walk" identify with the people who are in need. They do not simply talk about the situation. They join with the people in need to take action and do something to meet the needs and change the circumstances which create the problem. They assume responsibility and proceed to act.

The parable we deal with today puts into story form a somewhat similar distinction. The son in the parable who said yes to the request of the father to work in the vineyard but did not do it "talked the talk" but did not "walk the walk." The son who refused the father's request but later changed his mind and went to work in the vineyard "walked the walk."

Context

Context of the Church Year

We are in a series that would afford an opportunity to do five parables in succession if one so chose to do it. This is the third of the parables, with two more to follow. This parable and the next use the imagery of workers in the vineyard, as did the parable for the previous Sunday.

Context of the Gospel

The parables for today and for next Sunday are in Matthew 21. They follow an increasing crisis of conflict between Jesus and the religious leaders. They raise questions about his source of authority. He counters with a question about what they think about the authority of John the Baptist. They knew that if they said it was on his own authority, they would alienate the common people among whom John was very popular. If they granted him to have authority from heaven for his message, they could not very well deny Jesus the same authority.

The parables speak to the question of authority and call into question those who have the position of formal authority but do not necessarily carry it out in practice. Others may not have an office, but they perform the function which should be appropriate to the office.

The First Lesson. (Exodus 17:1-7) The people quarreled at Rephidim because they had no water to drink. Moses understood this to be a test of the Lord. They objected because they thought Moses had brought them into the desert where they and their livestock would die of thirst. Moses was then advised to go ahead of the people to Horeb where he struck his rod against a rock. He did so in the presence of the elders and the water flowed forth. That was the answer to the question he had posed as to whether the people were testing the Lord.

The Second Lesson. (Philippians 2:1-13) Paul asserts the authority of Jesus. The key is found in v. 9 where Paul, after describing the servant role of Jesus, says, "Therefore" and proceeds to assert his cosmic authority. He calls the Philippians to faithfulness in accepting the authority of Jesus over their lives.

Gospel. (Matthew 21:23-32) The passage gives the parable of the obedient and disobedient sons.

Psalm. (Psalm 78:1-4, 12-16) The Psalm ties together both the first lesson by reference to the events in Egypt and the Gospel lesson by pointing toward the technique of Jesus in using parables to make clear his teachings about the kingdom.

>Isaiah 5:1-7 — The song of the vineyard.
>
>Amos 6:6-8 — Justice, not sacrifice, desired by the Lord.
>
>Micah 6:6-8 — What the Lord requires beside sacrificial ceremonies.
>
>Matthew 7:21, Luke 6:46 — Saying Lord, but not obeying.
>
>Luke 3:12-13 — Tax collectors admonished by John the Baptist.
>
>Luke 7:37-50 — How Jesus forgave a prostitute.
>
>James 1:22-25 — Faith demonstrated by works.
>
>1 John 3:18 — Love not in word or speech, but in real deeds.

Content of the Pericope

The parable is unique to Matthew. The brief parable raises three important issues:

1. The significance of repentance that leads to obedience to God's will. The first son changes his mind. His actions are more important than his initial response.

2. The greater receptivity for change among those who are obviously sinners — tax collectors and prostitutes — than among those who are professional religionists. A sense of need is more likely to lead to repentance than a sense of already having arrived.

3. The kingdom is open to all. Entrance into the kingdom is not so much on the behavior or actions of the past or on profession of readiness to obey, but is dependent on readiness to act in obedience once the call is received. The readiness to act in response to God's will is evidence of true repentance.

Precis of the Parable

The owner of a vineyard had two sons. He told the first son to go and work in the vineyard. The son was rebellious and at first said he would not do it. Later he had a change of heart and actually did go to work.

The father went to the second son. He told him to go to work also. The second son seemed to be compliant. He said he would. But he never showed up in the vineyard. Jesus does not say whether his failure to do the father's bidding was because of rebellion, thoughtlessness or sheer laziness.

When Jesus asked his opponents who was the true son of the Father, they had to agree that the son who actually obeyed despite his first refusal was, of course, the real son. The one who seemed to be more compliant but did not do what he said he would was not the true son.

Jesus then makes application to the present situation, both in his own ministry of finding the tax collectors and prostitutes responsive to his call to repent and enter the kingdom and in the response to the preaching of John the Baptist.

Thesis: Repentance leading to obedience is more important than profession without corresponding deeds.

Theme: What counts with God is right action.

Key Words in the Parable

1. "Think." (v. 28) Jesus signals that he has something important to say. He wants his hearers to pay attention and consider the implications of what he is about to relate as it applies to the controversy at hand.

2. "Vineyard." (v. 28) As noted in an earlier parable, the vineyard imagery was already used in the Old Testament as the place where God calls his people to labor with him in the midst of the world. It is where his sons and daughters work in order to receive the reward of his kingdom.

3. "He Changed his Mind." (v. 29) Repentance means a change of direction. It is more than just being sorry for past behavior. It means now moving to do what earlier was refused.

4. "Sir." (v. 30) The term indicates respect for the father. The actual term in the Greek is *kyrie* which normally would be translated Lord. This is the euphemism used instead of God at that time. It clearly indicates that Jesus intended the father to be an image of God. He indirectly implies a judgment against those who too easily mouthed the expression but did not translate it into real understanding and submission to God's will.

5. "Kingdom of God." (v. 31) This is not a typical expression for Matthew. He usually referred to the kingdom of heaven. To refer to the kingdom of God would be more typical of the term used by Luke.

6. "Ahead of You." (v. 31) "You" refers to the opponents of Jesus who used flattering address yet really were seeking to trap him. They wanted to find a reason to accuse him of some religious error. Their questions were not sincere in seeking to understand him and respond to his message.

7. "The Tax Collectors and the Prostitutes." (vv. 31 and 32) The tax collectors and the prostitutes would be the stereotypical images of persons whom everyone would assume to be sinners and disloyal to God. They are chosen to make the contrast as graphic as possible for the hearers of the parable.

Contemplation

Insights

1. Orthodoxy or Orthopraxy. The parable of the two sons would seem to come down on the side of orthopraxy (right action) as opposed to right teachings or doctrines (orthodoxy.) The son who seemed to reject the father's request but did the work is the one who is right. In the context of the situation in which the parable is placed, the people who had been obvious sinners were more approved than those whose major occupation was to study and teach the religion. It is not enough to know the right ideas or doctrines. They have to be acted upon. Indeed, it is probably true that right doctrines are not really understood until they are put into practice.

2. True Repentance. Some people seem quite ready to say, "I'm sorry," if they fail to do something or if they do something that is wrong. Nevertheless, they continue in the same habits. A person habitually ran behind schedule, showing up late for work assignments, for committee meetings, in submitting reports. Each time the person would say "I'm sorry." What was wanted was not apologies but performance. True repentance does not mean only asking to be excused for behavior; it is only true repentance when a change in practice accompanies the apology.

3. Life Witness. A strong Christian witness depends on integrity between the profession of faith and the life of the believer. The hypocrisy of those who claim to be followers of Christ and the denial of it in their life styles is one of the main obstacles to persons coming to a church or for young people to leave the church. A life lived as a serious attempt to accord with the example and teachings of Christ is one of the strongest invitations to others to become followers of him as Lord. Without the joining of faith and works which flow from it, the appeal to others is hollow.

4. No Sinner Excluded. Jesus in his ministry was open to all persons. He saw people in sin not as persons to be avoided, condemned or rejected. He saw them as people in need and he acted to meet the need. He did not judge them according to the label given to them by his society but according to their potential when redeemed by the grace of God. He was more impressed by the possibilities of those with obvious needs, such as the tax collectors and the prostitutes, responding with repentance and a changed life than those who thought themselves already to be religious.

5. Resolving Conflicts. People use a variety of mechanisms for resolving conflicts, some more useful than others. The chief priests and the elders in this instance tried confronting Jesus. Confrontation may be a useful mechanism if persons are interested in resolving the conflict. In this case they were not interested in a genuine attempt to deal with the conflict but were seeking to trap Jesus so they could arrest him. He uses another mechanism when he expanded the conflict by introducing the question of the authority of John the Baptist. This is sometimes called issue proliferation.

The chief priests and the elders chose another mechanism at that point. They decided to avoid the conflict. Jesus tried another mechanism. He challenged them to change their minds. In a dispute where people have differences of religious beliefs, ideologies, philosophies, or values, a conflict can only be resolved fully by some party having a change of belief. When people come to agreement, they use the mechanism of reconciliation in which the parties achieve unity and no conflict exists.

In the case here neither was willing to change and so the conflict was postponed and came back later in a worse form. The leaders decided to use the mechanism of elimination of the opponent. Only, as we know, it did not really resolve the conflict because of the resurrection of Christ.

Homily Hints

1. Creeds and Deeds. (vv. 28-30) Here the issue is not whether or not works lead to salvation. The issue is whether belief is real unless it manifests itself in action which follows from it.
    A. Belief Expressed in Words
    B. Belief Expressed in Works
    C. Validating Words with Works

2. The Changed Mind. (vv. 29, 32) How does a person come to a change through repentance? Develop the stages of the process.

A. Acknowledging Need. A person has to acknowledge wrongdoing before repentance occurs.

B. Rejecting the Past. A person needs to give up behaviors which may have seemed satisfying and satisfactory previously.

C. Turn to the New Future. A person becomes a new person when empowered by the Holy Spirit to move into the future as a new beginning.

3. The First in the Kingdom. (v. 31) Contrast the conventional views about who is a good person with the way Jesus would give priority.

A. The World View. Those who lord it over others, who control and dominate, are usually looked upon as number one.

B. Jesus' View. Jesus gives priority to servanthood as the measure of who is number one.

C. A Reverse Priority. The kingdom of heaven goes contrary to conventional wisdom about priorities.

D. Your Response

4. True Children of God. (vv. 28-32) The question to each person by this parable is whether we identify ourselves with the first son or the second son.

A. The Demand of Obedience

B. The Claim of Sonship

C. The Real Test in Behavior

5. Talkers and Doers. (vv. 28-31) Some people talk about needs. Others proceed to meet the need or solve the problem. Some people are so busy doing many things they never stop to ask if they are meeting real needs or doing the most important thing.

A. All Talk, No Action

B. All Doing, No Reflection

C. A Rhythm of Talking and Doing

Contact

Points of Contact

1. Many people live with tension between what they hear and confess in church on Sunday and how they respond to pressures other days of the week. They can be challenged to ask whether they show they are sons and daughters of the Father in the daily work and walk.

Children show their kinship to their parents in many physical characteristics. Christians show their kinship in how they behave. Their character should conform to the God they have seen in Jesus Christ. When it does, they are children of God and it shows.

2. The church should have a different appreciation of people than what the usual standards of the world are. A church needs to ask if it would be embarrassed if certain persons would be included in its membership. The background of the person should not be a barrier to membership. A church that only finds persons of a certain socio-economic status or a particular ethnic and racial heritage acceptable is not answering the question which Jesus posed to the chief priests and elders. It would seem that even the test of assent to a particular creed is not the crucial question. The criteria suggested are the actions that show a willingness to obey God's will as they understand it and to do God's work to which they are called.

3. People need to be confronted with the question of what authority Jesus has for them. If they acknowledge that Jesus is Lord as well as Savior, their lives should show it in their actions. They should be doing the work of the kingdom he proclaimed and lived. The final test of the acceptance of the authority of Jesus as coming from heaven and not from human sources is in the conformity of life and works to his commands and example.

Points to Ponder

1. Does the church spend too much of its efforts and attention on those who have already committed themselves to

Christ? Should it rather seek out those who are sinners in need? Jesus did not invest most of his time with the religious community. He reached out to people in need and invited them to come into the kingdom. Does this parable challenge the church today to do likewise?

2. Who is the good person? Jesus did not seem to be much impressed by the status of persons. He was more concerned with the direction of their movement. Tax collectors or prostitutes who were trying to change the direction of their lives were given more approval by Jesus than the religious leaders who had high social status. Is the process of change in life more important in judging who is a good person than where the person happens to stand at a given moment?

3. How do people change? Two factors may be most effective in bringing people to change. One is an awareness of some inconsistency between their present value system and what they come to realize is a better one. The second is the presence of role models which they come to accept as a better example for them to emulate than they find in their own lives. Can we attract them to change by confronting them with the highest values embodied in the kingdom of God and giving them living role models which show what Christ can mean as a model to emulate?

4. How do you make faith operational? What one person described as "stratospheric theology" needs to be translated into understandable terms for the laity. It is important to think seriously and carefully about the Christian faith. It is more important to demonstrate it in daily living. Is the end of theology just to have correct ideas about the important issues, or should it be to issue in a living that helps fulfill the prayer "Your kingdom come on earth as it is in heaven"?

5. The chief priests and the elders were very careful to observe all the proper rituals and ceremonies. How do you prevent such religious practices from becoming ends in themselves and a substitute for a dynamic religious life that permeates all of a person's actions? How do you make the rituals and ceremonies not an empty formalism but a preparation to say yes to the request of the Father to work in his kingdom?

Illustrative Materials

1. Down and Outers or Up and Outers. Eugenia Price began her Christian ministry working among the alcoholics and homeless people on the south side of the Chicago loop, the so-called "Skid Row." Later she lived on the near north side of Chicago, the so-called Gold Coast. She observed that it was harder to bring the "up and outers" of the Gold Coast to Christian commitment than it was among the "down and outers" of skid row. She might have paraphrased Jesus by saying that the alcoholics and homeless would go into the kingdom ahead of the socially elite and business personnel of Chicago.

2. Perform or Resign. Ryne Sandberg was an all-star second baseman for the Chicago Cubs. In mid-June 1994, he suddenly and unexpectedly resigned. The year before he had signed a four-year contract for $28 million. He had over three years yet to go on the contract, which meant he could earn $18 million more just by continuing to play. No one was pressuring him to quit.

Sandberg quit because his batting average at .238 had dropped over 50 points from his lifetime average of .289. He also had lost some of his enthusiasm for playing. He said, "I am not the type of person who can be satisfied with anything less than my very best effort and my very top performance... And I am certainly not the type of person who can ask the Cubs organization and the Chicago Cubs' fans to pay my salary when I am not happy with my mental approach and my performance."

3. Think! Someone has observed that five percent of the people think; ten percent of the people think they think; 85 percent of the people would rather die than think.

A speaker at a conference observed that the only thing harder to open than the plastic pack of peanuts given to passengers on an airline is the human mind to a new idea.

4. Preaching or Social Action. The debate was over which was more important: Proclamation of the word in evangelism and missions or doing relief work and developing and working for social justice. A pastor said, "They are like a pair of pants: Singular at the top in the Gospel, but plural at the bottom in practice."

5. Faith Expressed in Works. A young pastor and his wife, a nurse, worked in a fairly conservative inner-city church. Many people in the congregation did not like his liberal theology. They could not, however, fault the couple because of the way in which they showed a deep concern for the problems and needs of the people in the neighborhood. He worked hard to try to find jobs for the church members. He visited them in their homes. He organized activities for the young people. His wife visited the sick in the community and offered help when they were incapacitated. Both were much respected and held in affection by those to whom they ministered unselfishly.

10. Wicked Tenants

Matthew 21:33-46

"Listen to another parable. There was a landowner who planted a vineyard, put a fence around it, dug a wine press in it, and built a watchtower. Then he leased it to tenants and went to another country. [34]When the harvest time had come, he sent his slaves to the tenants to collect his produce. [35]But the tenants seized his slaves and beat one, killed another, and stoned another. [36]Again he sent other slaves, more than the first; and they treated them in the same way. [37]Finally he sent his son to them, saying, 'They will respect my son.' [38]But when the tenants saw the son, they said to themselves, 'This is the heir; come, let us kill him and get his inheritance.' [39]So they seized him, threw him out of the vineyard, and killed him. [40]Now when the owner of the vineyard comes, what will he do to those tenants?" [41]They said to him, "He will put those wretches to a miserable death, and lease the vineyard to other tenants who will give him the produce at the harvest time."

[42]Jesus said to them, "Have you never read in the scriptures: 'The stone that the builders rejected has become the cornerstone; this was the Lord's doing, and it is amazing in our eyes'?

[43]"Therefore I tell you, the kingdom of God will be taken from you and given to a people that produces the fruits of the kingdom. [44]The one who falls on this stone will be broken to pieces; and it will crush anyone on whom it falls."

137

*⁴⁵When the chief priests and the Pharisees
heard his parables, they realized that he was speaking
about them. ⁴⁶They wanted to arrest him, but they feared
the crowds, because they regarded him as a prophet.*

The parable is found in Mark 12:1-12 and Luke 20:9-19 as
well as in Matthew. Question is raised as to whether the parable is
given in its original form as told by Jesus or whether it is embel-
lished with additional details from the experience of the church
after the death and resurrection of Jesus.

The issue is in part concerned with one's belief about pre-
dictive prophecy. Did Jesus have prescience about what would
happen to the church after his death, or did the writers of the parable adapt it to conform to events which they experienced and that
fit with the original parable?

The parable as it is given can be used as an allegory. Its
details can be assigned to events and parties in the Old Testament.
The concluding verses may be given added strength if the gospels
according to Matthew and Luke were written later than 70 A.D. as
many authorities believe. In 70 A.D. Jerusalem was conquered by
the Romans after an attempted revolt and the temple was destroyed.
After that happened Christianity was increasingly considered as
separate from Judaism and no longer just as a sect within Judaism.
Thus possibly v. 43 in Matthew and v. 18 in Luke which are not in
Mark (who probably wrote the gospel prior to 70) were added by
the writers in light of the events that happened about the time that
they wrote their Gospel account.

Context

Context of the Gospel

The parable is another that draws upon a parallel between
the image of a vineyard and the kingdom of God. It continues the
response of Jesus to the question about his authority and his rejection by the Chief Priests and scribes.

It was increasingly evident to Jesus that he and his followers would have to organize separately from the established institutions of Judaism. He no doubt was disappointed with the developments and still hoped that he could persuade the leadership to change and accept his vision of the kingdom. With the intensifying of the opposition, he held less and less hope that such would be possible and believed that his death was imminent, as in fact was the case.

Context of the Lectionary

The First Lesson. (Exodus 20:1-4,7-9,12-20) The reading gives the essentials of the ten commandments. This is probably the fence referred to in Matthew 21:33. Laws set boundaries for behavior in a way similar to fences which set boundaries to prevent trespassing of territory.

The Second Lesson. (Philippians 3:4b-14) Paul gives his autobiographical confession of his background in Judaism and his commitment to follow Christ despite the suffering it has cost him.

Gospel. (Matthew 21:33-46) The parable is of the wicked tenants who tried to obtain possession of the vineyard by destroying the servants and the son who were sent to collect the return due the owner from it.

Psalm. (Psalm 19) The psalm is an affirmation of the response of the earth to the Creator. The psalmist proceeds to assert the value of the law and the reward offered to those who observe it faithfully.

Context of Related Scriptures

Psalm 118:22 ff. — The stone that the builder rejected.
Isaiah 8:14-15 — A reference to the stone of stumbling upon which many will fall and be broken.

Daniel 2:34-35 — The stone that breaks an idol and becomes a mountain to fill the whole earth.

Malachi 2:7-8 — False priests by their instruction cause
persons to stumble.

Matthew 23:2-3 — The scribes and Pharisees do not practice what they teach.

Matthew 23:34 — Prophets sent are killed, flogged and
pursued.

John 15:1-7 — The image of the true vine and the vine
growing.

Acts 4:11 — Another use of the stone that was rejected.

Romans 9:32-33 — Paul refers to the stone over which
people stumble.

Hebrews 11:36-38 — Mention of the prophets who were
stoned, sawn in two and killed by the sword.

Content

Characteristics of the Parable

The parable as noted is more of an allegory than the
usual parables of Jesus. The characters and the events have
reference to the history of Israel as interpreted by either Jesus
or the early church.

It is clear that God is the owner of the vineyard. That he
was an absentee landlord might suggest that he was not perceived
as active in the intertestamental period as he was earlier. The writers of the New Testament understood time to have certain propi-
tious moments when God revealed himself in history through
mighty acts. The time was ripe for harvest when John the Baptist
and Jesus appeared on the scene.

In the interim between the old and new covenantal periods
the people of Israel were left to tend the vineyard. They were the
tenants. They were accountable to God to produce fruits of the
kingdom. Repeatedly through Israel's history the people failed
and had to be redeemed. The history of the Old Testament is re-
plete with a cycle of redemption by God, apostasy by the people,

judgment through the events of history which brought them to repentance, and restoration through God's intervening grace.

The servants who were sent from time to time to call the tenants of the vineyard to accountability were the prophets. The various servants in the parable sent to call the tenants to accountability represent the prophets of the Old Testament. A distinction was made between the earlier prophets, such as Isaiah and Jeremiah, and the latter or minor prophets. Tradition says that Isaiah was killed by being sawn asunder. Jeremiah was mistreated in various ways.

Jesus the son is the heir to the vineyard. The slightly different wording of Matthew when compared to Mark may refer to the crucifixion of Jesus outside of Jerusalem. Matthew says the son was cast out of the vineyard and killed whereas Mark says he was killed and then cast out.

Matthew also elaborates the consequences of what the owner did when he came. He first puts the words in the mouth of Jesus' opponents when Jesus posed the question of what the owner would do. Mark simply has the question posed and answered. Matthew adds that the tenants will suffer a miserable death, perhaps aware of what happened in Jerusalem in 70 A.D. Matthew adds v. 43 to reassert that the kingdom would be taken away from his opponents and given to a nation producing the fruits of the kingdom. That other nation would be the church which included Gentiles as well as Jews.

Precis of the Parable

The story line of the parable proceeds along lines which draw on two images from the Old Testament which appear frequently in the New Testament. The first is that of the vineyard. An absentee landlord, which was common enough at the time to be well known, left tenants in charge of the vineyard. They were sharecroppers who would give a portion of the crop as payment of rent to the owner.

The tenants conspired to take over the vineyard, assuming either that the landlord was so far removed that he would never return or anticipating that he would die in his absence. When his servants came to collect the fruits due the owner they killed them so that they could keep all the fruit for themselves. That happened repeatedly in Israel's history.

Finally the owner sent his son, assuming the tenants would not have the audacity to kill his heir. The tenants saw this as their opportunity to gain full ownership of the vineyard. If they killed the son, no heirs would survive and they would become the outright owners of the land.

The tenants misjudged the owner. He returned and wreaked judgment on the tenants. He put them to death and replaced them with new, more faithful tenants.

The second image from the Old Testament is that of the stone of stumbling. The very stone which they regarded as a scandal becomes the cornerstone of a new building. That was perceived by the early church as the replacement of the destroyed temple. Jesus became the cornerstone of the new temple. It was the church, a living temple composed of believers, and not a physical temple confined to Jerusalem.

Thesis: Persons reject the kingdom and its agents at their own peril.

Theme: The death of God's servants does not frustrate God's purposes but brings punishment to those responsible for it.

Key Words in the Parable

1. "Landowner." (v. 33) God is the landowner. All the earth and its riches are his. Persons occupying the earth are only tenants, not owners. They are accountable to God for their use of the earth.

2. "Fence." (v. 33) The limit set to God's kingdom is the law which was given to Moses. The law established the boundaries for Israel as God's people.

3. "Dug a Wine Press." (v. 33) A wine press was used to extract the juice from the grapes. Thus the product of the fruit could be stored. The press was set up so that as the grapes were pressed the juice ran down to the bottom where it was collected and saved.

4. "Watchtower." (v. 33) Some understand the watchtower to be the temple which was to safeguard the teaching and observance of the law. It may also have included the synagogue.

5. "Leased it to Tenants." (v. 33) An absentee landowner in Palestine would retain ownership of the vineyard but would lease it to others on a sharecropping basis.

6. "Sent His Slaves ... Other Slaves." (vv. 34 and 36) The prophet's function is to speak forth the word of God. It is likely that the various slaves were the former and latter prophets of the Old Testament period.

7. "Collect His Produce." (v. 34) The usual arrangement was for the landowner to receive one-quarter of the crop at the time of harvest. This was the rent paid by the tenants.

8. "Sent His Son." (v. 37) Jesus did not generally ascribe to himself the title of the Son of God. He more frequently referred to himself as the Son of Man. The church, however, did call him the Son of God and understood him to be sent by God.

9. "Other Tenants." (v. 41) The other tenants were the church which included both Gentile and Jewish Christians.

10. "Stone ... Rejected." (v. 42) Earlier the stone that was rejected was the message of the prophets. Now it becomes Christ who was rejected and cast down. After his resurrection he became the center of the church.

11."Becomes the Cornerstone." (v. 42) The cornerstone

holds the building together. It may have been a keystone in the middle of an arch rather than the corner that ties two walls together. In any event it is crucial to the structure. Without it the edifice would collapse.

Contemplation

Insights

1. The Earth is the Lord's. The earth was established by God with conditions necessary to support life. Some environmentalists blame the Judeo-Christian doctrines for the exploitation of the earth which results in the depletion of natural resources and degradation of the environment through pollution and other abuses. They contend that the belief that persons are to have dominion over the earth allowed these actions. It can be argued, however, that the Judeo-Christian belief is not that persons are to have unlicensed dominion over the earth. They are to exercise stewardship over it. They are temporary tenants who are to tend it as a vineyard. If cared for properly it will produce abundant fruit and sustain life. They are not to abuse or misuse it for immediate gain at the expense of future yield. The environment is created by God with amazing recuperative capacity. Good tenants assure that the bounds set on the productivity of the earth do not exceed its possibilities of continuing, life-sustaining productivity.

2. Freedom to Reject. Persons are created with the freedom to reject God. They may reject his being and his message. The rejection is not without consequences however. The universe has a moral structure. If persons assume that they are in complete control and run the world according to their own interests and contrary to God's will, they suffer the effects of their actions. Eventually the flouting of God's will brings destruction, and the ultimate consequence is a miserable death, worse than the death of the physical body. It is to miss the very meaning of life itself.

3. Martyrdom. It is the nature of sin to hate anything which judges it. To try to deny the message of judgment, those who operate by self-interest, hoping thereby to escape the message, will try to destroy the messenger. The true prophet who speaks God's words of warning and judgment threatens people who do not want to hear it. Because prophets deal with issues of ultimate values, the attack against them will be most ferocious. That is why religious wars and persecution of those who profess differing religious values are often characterized by their ferocity. If the values were not so important they would not arouse people so. Those who stand for values of ultimate worth and meaning should not be surprised if martyrdom is the consequence. It has been so in the past and continues to be so.

4. Constant Reformation. When an institution gets so bad, it either must be reformed or it will be destroyed and replaced. The passing of the gospel from a Jewish exclusiveness to a Christian inclusiveness and universality is one example of the need for reformation or replacement. The sixteenth century Reformation is another example of a need for change and the passing of responsibilities to others when it appeared that the medieval church was no longer open to the drastic changes needed. As society was changing, new conditions required new adaptations. New economic forces, new means of communication and new political realities all led people to have a different understanding of religious demands and this led to the Reformation.

The Reformation is not something simply to be celebrated. It is a reminder that the church needs constant reformation or it will cease to be a faithful servant. The church as a human institution as well as a spiritual organism may be subject to the tendency of all human institutions. They become extensions of self interests. When they do, they either must go through a painful reformation or be supplanted by others which are vitalized by the Holy Spirit and produce fruits of the kingdom more faithfully.

1. Produce of the Harvest. (vv. 34, 41) What does God expect as our response to his bounty toward us? What kind of harvest should workers in his vineyard produce?

A. A Goodly Life. In personal life the Christian should manifest the works of the Holy Spirit.

B. A Faithful Church. Support and encouragement of the church in its fullest extension is another important fruit.

C. Social and Economic Justice. Working to bring God's kingdom into being in the world at large is another way to produce fruit for the harvest.

2. Treating His Slaves. (vv. 35-36) Prophetic voices often lead to intense opposition because of their challenge to our apathy and comfort. They call us to awaken to needs for change and to undertake tasks that are difficult and may be dangerous.

A. Heed Their Voice. Listen receptively.

B. Test Their Message. Use the plumbline of scripture to discern the true from the false.

C. Tolerate Their Zeal. Do not be too quick to condemn or reject that which challenges the status quo, the conventional wisdom, our own power and privilege.

D. Free Them for the Work. They are worthy of their hire.

3. Respect My Son. (v. 37) Many persons did not respect Jesus in the days of his flesh. Many today also reject him without really knowing and understanding him.

A. Know Him. Enter into his life through the scriptures and personal encounter of him.

B. Grow into Him. Let his teachings and example permeate and transform our lives.

C. Show Him. Empowered by his Spirit, act in all situations as he would act today to show others who he is.

4. Responsible Tenants. (v. 41) This is an opportunity for a stewardship sermon.

A. Use of Personal Gifts
B. Use of Wealth
C. Use of the Earth

5. A Stumbling Stone or the Cornerstone? (v. 42) Contemporary society often finds the particularity of following Christ a scandal. They find the idea of the resurrection of Christ an impossibility. The relativism and toleration of diversity rejects the exclusivity of Christian claims as unacceptable.
A. Is Christ Your Stumbling Stone?
B. The Uniqueness of Christ
C. The Centrality of Christ
D. Life Needs a Cornerstone

6. Amazing in Our Eyes. (v. 43) Worship helps to refocus our wonder and awe at the amazing works of God.
A. Amazed at God's Acts in History
B. Amazed at God's Acts in Persons
C. Amazed at God's Acts in Today's World

Contact

Points of Contact

1. Human beings want to find meaning in their lives. They are aware that they have some choice and some responsibility for who they are and what they become. Psychiatrists meet people with deep anxiety. They have a free-floating fear. It is not directed to a specific cause of fear. It arises from the fear that they are responsible for some cosmic meaning that they have missed. They may fear that they are rejected by God when the real cause may be their rejection of God, or at least an unwillingness to put their trust in him. Finding God's favor and responding with commitment may relieve that anxiety.

2. God does not approach people only once and give them opportunity to respond. He is persistent and makes his approach through various agents and means. Christians need various occasions

147

for renewing their faith and commitment as they meet God's repeated actions. The approach of God may come in various ways at different stages in life. It may come in the confrontation to decide on personal philosophy in adolescence. It may come in a vocational choice in early adulthood. It may come in career shifts throughout life. It may come again as one assumes responsibility for a family. It may come in awareness of social needs or injustices in the world. It may come at retirement and the approaching end of life. Any crisis may call for a new choice for returning to God fruits of the kingdom.

3. The battle against evil is not just between parties, as between the wicked tenants and the landowner. It is also within each of us. Each person has what is described as a dark side. People are tempted to use means to obtain ends that are evil, both in the means and the ends. Such means and ends need to be branded for what they are. Unless they are repented they lead to destruction. God's patience and mercy have limits. The limits are set by the human rejection of God's overtures and not by the character of God.

Points to Ponder

1. Punishment. The parable raises the issue of the nature of God's punishment for disobedience and rejection of his will and his agents. Is it an arbitrary act of wrath or is it so built into the structure of being that the consequences follow as an inevitable and natural consequence of our actions? Is the punishment immediate and direct, or is it only evident as a result of a process that takes time to work out? Or is the final punishment outside of history, either at a person's death or at some final outcome of history?

2. Other Nations. The nineteenth and early twentieth century were characterized as an age of missionary activity on the part of the European and North American churches. In the latter half of this century mission efforts have declined among many of these churches. Mission giving has decreased so that mission budgets have had to be reduced. Fewer people volunteer to devote their lives as missionaries. Some attribute the decrease to the spending of local churches on their own projects: large buildings, more facilities, more comfortable furnishings, more professional staff because fewer volunteer to provide services. Is it possible that the next major missionary movement will come from third world churches that have a vitality and enthusiasm for the gospel? Already some third world churches are sending missionaries to Europe and North America.

3. Prophets or Fanatics. It is often difficult to distinguish the fanatic from the true prophet. It is important that persons make the distinction. The test of the fanatic is the person who is obsessed with himself. He feeds his own desires and thirst for power and control. If someone makes a claim to being a prophet but acts contrary to the spirit of Christ he must be seen as a fanatic and not a true prophet. Unquestioning loyalty should not be given to the fanatic, no matter how charming or persuasive the fanatic may seem. Final loyalty belongs to Christ alone and not to any human leader, no matter how charismatic the leader may be.

4. Toleration of Diversity. A difficult stance to maintain is a toleration of diversity when a person is deeply committed to beliefs and loyalties. A fine line separates understanding and accepting persons who seem to transgress values held most dear and embracing the values of those persons as valid. The trick of opposing wickedness perpetrated without taking upon oneself the destruction of the perpetrator requires a disciplined adherence to the respect for the life of every person regardless of his or her actions. It also requires a trust that God is the final vindicator of real values.

Illustrative Materials

1. Given to Others. Saint Francis of Assisi (1181-1226) had a dream in which a church was in danger of splitting in two. He saw himself called upon to hold it together. He devoted himself to try to prevent the breach in the church from leading to its destruction in an age of rapid change. His life and teachings led to the founding of a new order within the church, though it was not his intention to split the church. He did revitalize Christianity in his area through his teaching and that of his followers. He helped to maintain the unity of the medieval church for another two or three centuries.

John Wesley felt the church of his day was not ministering to the needs of the people. He set out to make changes. He traveled and preached incessantly. He did not intend to establish a new denomination. His followers met in chapels rather than churches originally. One finds many Methodist chapels in England. Nevertheless, he did become the founder of Methodism which split from the Anglican or Episcopalian Church.

In a similar way George Fox thought that the churches of his day were corrupted. His followers did not seek to found institutions, which he felt were part of the problem. So they used meeting houses and called themselves the Society of Friends rather than a church. The Society of Friends also eventually became a new denomination and developed their own characteristic institutions.

2. Modern Martyrs. Those who oppose the evils in society and vested interests still may be victims of the wickedness they oppose. Mahatma Gandhi practiced nonviolence and worked for reconciliation with those whom he opposed. He was assassinated by a fanatic from his own religion who thought he betrayed it in trying to overcome the violence between the Hindu and Moslem populations after independence of India from Great Britain was granted.

Martin Luther King, Jr., practiced and advocated Christian love and nonviolence in his struggle for civil rights. He was stabbed and almost killed by a black woman. Later he was assassinated for his beliefs and actions for civil rights, economic justice and opposition to the war in Vietnam.

It is reported that more Christian missionaries were buried in Algeria than converts were made from Muhammadanism to Christianity in that country.

3. Sense of Doom. Two men in their late adolescence and early adulthood had to be treated for mental illness because of their strong sense of doom. They came out of the treatment with a strong commitment to help the mentally ill. Clifford Beers became the founder of the Committee on Mental Hygiene which was a major force for improvement of conditions in mental hospitals. Anton Boisen became a leading figure in the pastoral care movement.

4. Misplaced Freedom. George Santayana, a Spanish philosopher, is reported to have said that if everyone does what he wills, nobody gets what he wants.

5. Fanaticism. Someone has defined a fanatic as one who can't change his mind and won't change the subject!

11. The King's Wedding Feast

Matthew 22:1-14

Once more Jesus spoke to them in parables, saying: [2]*"The kingdom of heaven may be compared to a king who gave a wedding banquet for his son.* [3]*He sent his slaves to call those who had been invited to the wedding banquet, but they would not come.* [4]*Again he sent other slaves, saying, 'Tell those who have been invited: Look, I have prepared my dinner, my oxen and my fat calves have been slaughtered, and everything is ready; come to the wedding banquet.'* [5]*But they made light of it and went away, one to his farm, another to his business,* [6]*while the rest seized his slaves, mistreated them, and killed them.* [7]*The king was enraged. He sent his troops, destroyed those murderers, and burned their city.* [8]*Then he said to his slaves, 'The wedding is ready, but those invited were not worthy.* [9]*Go therefore into the main streets, and invite everyone you find to the wedding banquet.'* [10]*Those slaves went out into the streets and gathered all whom they found, both good and bad; so the wedding hall was filled with guests.*

[11]*"But when the king came in to see the guests, he noticed a man there who was not wearing a wedding robe,* [12]*and he said to him, 'Friend, how did you get in here without a wedding robe?' And he was speechless.* [13]*Then the king said to the attendants, 'Bind him hand and foot, and throw him into the outer darkness, where there will be weeping and gnashing of teeth.'* [14]*For many are called, but few are chosen."*

153

Context

Context of the Lectionary

The First Lesson. (Exodus 32:1-14) The passage recounts the experience of the people of Israel in the wilderness when Moses had gone up the mountain of Sinai. They assumed that he was not returning. They appealed to Aaron for a god to lead them. He got from the people all the gold of their jewelry and from that produced the golden calf. The people proceeded with an orgy of worship. Moses came down and discovered what was happening. In his anger he shattered the tablets which contained the ten commandments. Moses then had to forestall the wrath of God who was inclined to blot out the people for their idolatry. Only Moses' pleading and willingness also to be blotted out turned aside the judgment upon the people.

The Second Lesson. (Philippians 4:1-9) Paul in his concluding message to the Philippians gives some specific instructions for members of the church. He also admonishes the church to continued faithfulness. He urges them to think on the things that will edify and strengthen them in such faithfulness. He assures them that it will bring genuine personal peace.

Gospel. (Matthew 22:1-14) The kingdom of heaven is compared to a wedding feast. Many are invited but refuse the invitation. Finally all kinds of guests are gathered to celebrate the great event.

Psalm. (Psalm 106:1-6, 19-23) The psalm begins with the call to praise the Lord, affirming his goodness and appealing to the Lord for deliverance and prosperity. It then goes on to acknowledge the sins of ancestors and recounts the episode of the golden calf as given in the first lesson.

Context of the Scriptures

The parable is part of the opposition which Jesus experienced

154

after the Triumphal Entry into Jerusalem and leading up to his crucifixion. It is part of several parables which explain the opposition
and the meaning of it. The opposition was primarily centered in
the officials of both the religious and the political community of
the time.

Matthew in writing the parable probably took some liber-
ties by embellishing it in light of some developments which make
the consequences of the opposition even more graphic, such as the
fall of Jerusalem to the Romans in 70 A.D. (See verse 7 about the
burning of the city.)

The parable may be compared to a somewhat similar passage in Luke 14:16-24.

Matthew	Luke
22:2 The kingdom of heaven may be compared to a king who gave a wedding banquet for his son.	14:16 Someone gave a great dinner and invited many.
22:3 He sent his slaves to call those who had been invited to the wedding, but they would not come.	14:17 At the time for the dinner he sent his slave to say to those who had been invited, "Come; for everything is ready now."
22:4 Again he sent other slaves, saying, "Tell those who have been invited: Look, I have prepared my dinner, my oxen and my fat calves have been slaughtered, and everything is ready; come to the wedding banquet."	
22:5 But they made light of it and went away, one to his farm, another to his business,	14:18 But they all alike began to make excuses. The first said to him, "I have bought a piece of land, and I must go out and see it; please accept my regrets."
22:6 while the rest seized his slaves, mistreated them, and killed them.	

155

22:7 The king was enraged. He sent his troops, destroyed those murderers, and burned their city.

22:8 Then he said to his slaves, "The wedding is ready, but those invited were not worthy.

22:9 Go therefore into the main streets, and invite everyone you find to the wedding banquet."

22:10 Those slaves went out into the streets and gathered all whom they found, both good and bad; so the wedding hall was filled with guests.

14:19 Another said, "I have bought five yoke of oxen, and I am going to try them out; please accept my regrets."

14:20 Another said, "I have just been married, and therefore I cannot come."

14:21 So the slave returned and reported this to his master. Then the owner of the house became angry and said to his slave, "Go out at once into the streets and lanes of the town and bring in the poor, the crippled, the blind, and the lame."

14:22 And the slave said, "Sir, what you ordered has been done, and there is still room."

14:23 Then the master said to the slave, "Go out into the roads and lanes, and compel people to come in, so that my house may be filled.

14:24 For I tell you, none of those who were invited will taste my dinner."

In the Matthean form we really have two parables (The Wedding Feast in 22:1-10 and The Wedding Robe in 22:11-14), whereas in Luke we have only one. If, as is generally assumed, parables in their original form had a single message, then the form recorded in Matthew has added features which allow for more than one message. One message deals with the rejection of the invitation to be part of the kingdom of heaven. The other is the rejection of those who are in the institutional expression of the kingdom of heaven, but are not worthy of it because of their impurities. Luke, on the other hand, is much simpler. It deals only with the excuses that persons make and the alternative offering of the kingdom when those most expected to respond do not accept the invitation. He

156

does elaborate more fully on the excuses which persons make. Luke apparently was not aware of the parable of the wedding robe. No parallels to Matthew's parable of the wedding robe exist elsewhere in the Gospels.

A feast figures as an expression elsewhere in the New Testament. John uses Jesus' participation in the wedding at Cana as a frontice piece for his gospel (John 2:1-11). Jesus was known and criticized for his feasting with sinners and tax collectors. Matthew 25:1-24 has the parable of the wise and unwise virgins who are included or excluded from the wedding due to their foresight or lack of preparation for it. A wedding feast is also one of the figures used in Revelation 14:7-9.

Content

Precis of the Pericope

Jesus' initial message was an invitation to enter the kingdom of heaven. He experienced repeated rejection of the invitation, particularly among the leaders of the spiritual community who should have been most receptive to it. Instead they were the ones who most opposed his ministry. The parable suggests that the invitation to enter the kingdom of heaven is similar to a king who holds a wedding feast. It was customary at the time to send a preliminary announcement of the approaching wedding to allow time to prepare for it. The parable suggests that God's earlier messengers, the prophets and probably also John the Baptist, were not received. Instead they were harassed and sometimes murdered. People continued "business as usual" despite the invitation to the great opportunity offered them. When the spiritual leaders reject the message and eliminate the messengers, the invitation is extended to others. Jesus probably referred to the sinners and tax collectors who responded readily. Matthew, writing some 40 years later, would have also understood it to apply to the Gentiles who were now part of the Christian church.

The second parable, Matthew 22:11-14, deals with a different problem that no doubt existed within the church. While the kingdom was open to the good and bad alike, persons who came into the church needed to lead lives worthy of the grace offered in the invitation. Membership in the church was not sufficient guarantee of salvation. A life had to conform to the demands of the kingdom once a person responded and claimed to be part of the kingdom.

Key Words in the Parable

1. "King." (v. 2) If the message is about the kingdom of heaven, then God is the King. It is reminiscent of the time in the Old Testament when Israel had no king but Yahweh, before the anointing of Saul as king under Samuel. Thus the wedding feast is no ordinary occasion. It would be a great honor to be invited to such a feast.

2. "Slaves." (v. 3) God uses servants to announce the invitation to accept his lordship and to enjoy the privileges and pleasures of honored guests. The prophets and preachers of former times would be those who had issued the invitation on behalf of God. Jesus took upon himself the role of the slave or servant (see Philippians 2:6, 7). In retrospect Matthew would also identify Jesus as among the slaves or servants who were slaughtered for carrying the message of invitation which was rejected.

3. "Invite Everyone ... to the Banquet." (v. 9) Jesus turned to the sinners and tax collectors with the invitation. He increasingly found receptivity among those persons while the spiritual leadership rejected his claims and his message. Again, Matthew, writing much later, would also recognize that Gentiles were responding in greater numbers than the Jews. Birthright did not guarantee being worthy of inclusion in the kingdom. The invitation has become universal, breaking the bounds of any national or ethnic particularism.

4. "Wearing a Wedding Robe." (v. 11) According to reports, the custom of the time was that persons waited around the king's palace, hoping to be invited into a feast. That would be especially true when a wedding feast was expected. Most persons would come in their finery, prepared for a wedding. Some, while waiting, apparently soiled their garments and did not have time to get them to the fuller to have them cleansed. By the time the gospel was composed, the church would have existed long enough that some would have slipped back into practices that were not proper for the kingdom. The parable warns that response to the invitation requires a proper life to accord with the participation in the kingdom. While the invitation is given without regard to whether one deserves it — "they found, both good and bad" (v. 10) — the joys of life in the kingdom are canceled if one does not prove worthy of being in the presence of the king.

5. "Weeping and Gnashing of Teeth." (v. 13) This expression is symbolic of the distress of those who have missed the meaning of real life in the kingdom. To be out of the presence of the king who is the source of life leaves persons in darkness. They then experience deep sorrow and regret at having missed the point of what life is all about.

Contemplation

The parable of the wedding feast has some problems associated with it. A danger which many face is to try to press every detail of the parable for meaning. It is best to keep in mind that a parable has a single point generally.

Question 1 — Is life in the kingdom of heaven one of joy? Too often persons view religion as negative and repressive. They know about the ten commandments with "Thou shalt not." They have probably been more impressed with the woes and threats of the gospel accounts than they are with the blessings. Jesus uses the image of the wedding feast to suggest the joy of life in the kingdom. It is contrasted with life outside the kingdom.

Question 2 — Who are the slaves sent by the King today? How can you discern who bears an authentic message of invitation? Do we still reject the messengers? David Koresh of Waco notoriety claimed to be a messiah, a chosen messenger of God. He attracted a number of dedicated followers. The federal government denied his claim. Earlier the Jonestown episode had a similar gathering that followed the leader from California to Guiana. Both of these situations ended in major tragedies. How do you validate who is an authentic messenger? Does the assassination of persons such as Martin Luther King, Jr., or Oscar Romero in El Salvador show that we still slaughter the bearers of God's invitation to the wedding feast? Some thought they were also false messengers who had to be eliminated.

Question 3 — To what extent does the parable justify an understanding of the anger and wrath of God? The destruction of Jerusalem was probably understood by Matthew and the early church as a consequence of the anger of God for the rejection and crucifixion of Jesus. Does God bring catastrophe on both the good and evil in a city such as Jerusalem as a manifestation of his anger? Someone suggested that the so-called "500 year flood" of the Mississippi might be related to the presence of increasing numbers of gambling boats on the river. Would God impose the suffering on such a wide area to make people aware of the consequence of such an evil?

How do you deal with the wrath of God in consigning the unrighteous to outer darkness with weeping and gnashing of teeth? Jesus seems to have presented both a loving, gracious, and forgiving God and an angry, wrathful God. How do you harmonize the two understandings of God's nature?

Question 4 — Is Christianity exclusive or inclusive? The conclusion of the double parable is "For many are called, but few are chosen" (v. 14). The invitation seems to be wide open and inclusive. Both the good and the bad are brought into the feast (v. 10). The one who is improperly attired is cast out to darkness with weeping and gnashing of teeth (v. 13). The kingdom has its demands.

In that sense it is exclusive. But the invitation is universal. The choice is left open to the person who may respond positively or negatively. While persons cannot earn entrance into the kingdom, they can prove themselves unworthy by their rejection of its demands once they have entered into it.

Question 5 — What is the relationship between the kingdom and the church? In contemporary society the church primarily enjoys acceptance and status. Not many Christians in democratic societies are suffering persecution. Rarely are preachers who proclaim the kingdom message slaughtered. Is it because the church has leavened the society, or is it because the church no longer presents the radical invitation to kingdom living? Has the church as it lives today made too easy an accommodation with the world around it? To be in the church do people not have to make real choices between the values of the kingdom and the values found in their work on the farm, in the factory, in business, in marrying and divorcing? Does the church no longer represent the coming of the kingdom, the wedding feast of God?

Question 6 — Is it true that many are called but few are chosen? (v. 14) Is Christianity only for the minority? Lawrence Kohlberg proposes that persons go through various stages of moral development: they begin with deference to superior power, obeying rules to avoid punishment; they move to self-gratification, proceed to mutual relationships, then to maintaining the social order, on to a social contract legalism, and finally orient to universal principles where they act according to what everyone everywhere should do at all times. Kohlberg suggests that most people operate at two levels, a lower and the next higher level.

Robert Coles, a child psychiatrist, disagrees with Kohlberg's proposal that movement from a lower level to the next higher is dependent upon stages of development that are age related. Coles does accept the general idea of the order of levels of moral action. Did Jesus recognize that few reach the highest stage of moral and spiritual development? All are confronted in life with the *call* for the highest level of moral and spiritual response, but in

161

reality only *few* accept the responsibility to act according to universal principles, that is to live in the kingdom of heaven.

Permanent Preaching Values of the Parable

1. The character of the King tells us something about the nature of the kingdom. It is in dealing with the character of the king as described in the parable that one should be careful about pressing the details of the story to far.

    A. *The character of the king.* The character of the king is more correctly portrayed in his readiness to offer the invitation to all, regardless of how worthy they are initially. The rage of the king is more a human characteristic than one of God. Nevertheless, God operates within a moral order which he created and life has consequences as suggested in the second part of the two parables.

    B. *Who is eligible for citizenship in the kingdom?* Here the grace of God is manifested in the openness of the invitation. It is not a privileged few determined by some arbitrary standard of wealth, power, ethnicity, or other human measures which decides who may come to the feast. All are welcome if they are willing to submit to God's gracious rule.

    C. *Requirements of citizenship?* Once in the kingdom, certain demands are placed upon its members. They live in obedience to the King whom they have accepted as Lord over their lives. Some have suggested, for example, that the Sermon on the Mount, especially the beatitudes, gives the qualifications of citizens in the kingdom.

    D. *The benefits of citizenship.* Enjoying the presence of the King and the largess of his grace is a primary benefit. One lives the festive life in the kingdom.

2. Who has been invited? The parable suggests who may be offered entrance into the kingdom and how the invitation is extended.

A. *The Gracious Invitation.* It is freely offered to all so that they may enter by grace.

B. *The Mediated Message.* The task of the messenger is to make the invitation to be attractive.

C. *Membership is Self-Selected.* While the offer is freely given and all are invited, persons must respond and be ready to participate in accordance with the nature of the wedding feast.

3. The Danger of Doing Good. The good may be an obstacle to the best. Persons should establish life priorities. The kingdom defines those priorities for true living.

A. The obstacle of work and family.

B. The obstacle of seeking results above all.

C. The obstacle of wrong means for good ends.

4. The Divine Diversity. God seeks to bring into union all manner of persons. The church should unite all people in a colorful array of diversity.

A. The church shatters economic barriers.

B. The church shatters racial barriers.

C. The church shatters gender barriers.

D. The church shatters cultural barriers.

Contact

The customs for a wedding feast in Jesus' day are different from our own. The preacher will need to translate the parable in a fashion that makes sense to people today. In a time when religious tolerance is generally promoted in western society the preacher will need to distinguish between tolerance of other persons and the recognition that the kingdom has demands that not everyone is willing to accept.

Two invitations were sent by the king. To the first invitation people declined because they were too preoccupied with the daily affairs of life. They were too busy with their routines to give heed to their spiritual lives. They were so concerned with making a living that they failed to make a life.

The people who were given the second invitation were not simply indifferent. They were in active rebellion against the king. They did not like the message so they killed the messengers.

The question to be posed is whether we miss the opportunity to enjoy the blessings of the kingdom because of indifference and neglect or are we engaged in active rebellion against the claims of the King on our life.

Illustrative Material

1. Religion a burden? An elderly Dutch couple toured American churches with a group. Toward the end of the trip as they sat resting while the other members looked at an impressive government building, the couple mused about their observations of churches of the same denomination in two different areas. They wondered why the members of the churches in one area seemed to be carried by their religion while the members of the same denomination in another area seemed to be carrying their religion as a burden.

2. Is joy excluded? A snowbound minister of a New England church decided that the only way he could get to the church on Sunday morning was to skate along a frozen river. He did so. After the morning service the elders asked him to wait while they had a consultation. Eventually they asked him to join them. The head of the session said they had some concern about his skating to church. He then told the pastor that they really had only one question, "Did you or did you not enjoy it?"

3. Doing wrong to do good. George DuPre of Calgary, Canada, reported that he had been a British agent in France during World War II. He was captured by the German Gestapo and underwent cruel torture. He refused to disclose the names of his colleagues in the French underground resistance movement. But the story proved to be a hoax. He confessed that it was not true but explained that he invented the story and others so that the Boy Scouts and other groups would listen to him with respect. He thought that by so doing he would be more able to influence them for good.

———————————

A woman who worked for an institution embezzled large sums of money. She never benefitted personally from the funds she took. She gave all the money to charitable organizations with whose purposes she had sympathy, but she did not have the resources to support them from her salary. Eventually she was discovered and had to pay the price for misuse of other's money.

4. Doing good for the wrong reason.

Now is my way clear, now is the meaning plain.
Temptation shall not come in this kind again.
The last temptation is the greatest treason:
To do the right deed for the wrong reason.
　　T. S. Eliot, "Murder In The Cathedral"

12. Prepared Or Not?

Matthew 25:1-13

"Then the kingdom of heaven will be like this. Ten bridesmaids took their lamps and went to meet the bridegroom. ²Five of them were foolish, and five were wise. ³When the foolish took their lamps, they took no oil with them; ⁴but the wise took flasks of oil with their lamps. ⁵As the bridegroom was delayed, all of them became drowsy and slept. ⁶But at midnight there was a shout, 'Look! Here is the bridegroom! Come out to meet him.' ⁷Then all those bridesmaids got up and trimmed their lamps. ⁸The foolish said to the wise, 'Give us some of your oil, for our lamps are going out.' ⁹But the wise replied, 'No! there will not be enough for you and for us; you had better go to the dealers and buy some for yourselves.' ¹⁰And while they went to buy it, the bridegroom came, and those who were ready went with him into the wedding banquet; and the door was shut. ¹¹Later the other bridesmaids came also, saying, 'Lord, lord, open to us.' ¹²But he replied, 'Truly I tell you, I do not know you.' ¹³Keep awake therefore, for you know neither the day nor the hour."

Weddings are wonderful! That is an expression you may hear frequently at the announcement of such an event. A lot of planning and expense usually go into making the event a special and joyous time. In our culture family and friends will travel long distances to be present at the ceremony.

Almost every culture has extensive traditions and customs surrounding a wedding. They underscore the importance of the

167

event. In our culture marriage is regulated by law. The state assumes that it has a stake in the proper arrangements and certification of a marriage. A wedding is an important and joyful community event.

The parable for today draws on the wedding ceremony and the traditions that surround it. Unhappy are those who for lack of adequate preparation miss the wedding. So are those who miss the kingdom of heaven and its joys.

Context

Context of the Lectionary

The parable and the following two come toward the end of the church year. It is fitting that the Gospel readings are three parables dealing with eschatology. They are three of the most familiar parables: the parable of the Wise and Foolish Virgins, the parable of the Talents and the parable of the Separation of the Sheep and Goats. Each of the parables deals with separation between those rewarded or accepted into the kingdom and those who are not.

Context of Matthew

The parable and the next two are placed in the last block of teaching materials in Matthew before the account of the final events of Jesus' life. They each give a likeness to the consequences of persons' response to the kingdom. The parable of the Wise and Foolish Virgins concludes with the rejection of those who do not prepare adequately for the coming of final events in history. The parable of the Talents speaks of wasted use of opportunities to act for the kingdom. The third portrays a final judgment between those who act on behalf of the kingdom in this world and those who do not act in accord with its character.

Context of a Wedding

Jesus frequently compares the kingdom to a glorious feast

168

of the king or of a wedding. In a Jewish wedding the bride waits at her father's house until the bridegroom comes to get her. She then accompanies him to his house where the ceremony takes place. On the way other participants in the wedding join the party and accompany the bridegroom and the bride to the festivities.

The time when the bridegroom would arrive to claim his bride was uncertain so that it would be a surprise. The bridegroom would come at night, so lamps were needed. Lamps were small clay vessels affixed to a staff. The vessels contained olive oil and had a wick for the flame. The vessels would need to be refilled from time to time as the people waited for the bridegroom to come.

Context of the Lectionary

The First Lesson. (Joshua 24:1-3a, 14-25) The passage is part of Joshua's farewell address to the people. He commits his house to serve the Lord. When the people responded that they will also, he warns them of what that means, especially if they do not keep their commitment. He proceeds to make a covenant and tells them the regulations that it implied.

The Second Lesson. (1 Thessalonians 4:13-18) The Thessalonians were disturbed that some had died and would not be alive for the second coming of Christ. Paul assures them that those asleep would not be treated differently from those still alive at Christ's return. The passage is related to today's Gospel reading by looking at death as sleep and the maidens sleeping while waiting for the bridegroom.

The Gospel. (Matthew 25:1-13) The parable tells of the contrast of the five maidens who give thought beforehand to be prepared. Five others are caught unprepared and miss the great event.

Psalm. (Psalm 78:1-7) The psalm underscores the need to transmit the faith to coming generations. Each new generation must remember what God has done and respond to him in obedience to his commands.

169

Psalm 45:14 — The virgins who are companions of the bride follow her.

Psalm 119:105 — The word is a lamp for guidance.

Matthew 5:15-16 — The works of the members of the kingdom are like a lamp that gives light to glorify the heavenly Father.

Mark 15:35-36 — An admonition to watch and not sleep.

2 Corinthians 11:2 — The church is described as a chaste virgin to be presented to Christ.

2 Peter 1:19 — The prophetic message served as a lamp shining in a dark place until the day dawns.

Revelation 19:7 — The marriage of the Lamb to the bride who is ready.

Revelation 21:2 — The new Jerusalem as a bride adorned for her husband.

Content

Content of the Parable

The parable uses a similarity between a wedding celebration and the kingdom of heaven. The point of the parable is the need for constant preparedness for the kingdom to break into daily existence. Some of the details of the parable lend themselves to further interpretation.

The use of the figure of the bridegroom makes an evident connection between the appearance of Jesus and the announcement of the presence of the kingdom. The early church with its expectation of an early return of Jesus to bring the kingdom to fulfillment understood the parable to speak of that coming event.

No mention is made of the bride. From the context a bride is self-evident. Who then are the ten maidens who waited for the coming of the wedding party? Were they the contemporary parties? The wise maidens might be the disciples who were prepared to answer the call of Jesus and follow him. The foolish maidens could be the chief priests, the scribes and the Pharisees who expected a messiah to come and deliver Israel from its oppressors yet they were not prepared to respond either to John the Baptist or Jesus when they proclaimed the presence of the kingdom of God.

The joy of the wedding feast is contrasted with those who were left on the outside in the dark looking into the house where the festivities were in process.

Precis of the Parable

A wedding ceremony is anticipated. A group of ten maidens were awaiting the event, expecting to be part of the wedding party. They had their lamps chasing away the darkness of the night. The bridegroom lingered. Finally about midnight the word is spread that the bridegroom and bride are about to arrive.

Half of the five maidens suddenly realize that their lamps are flickering low and are about to die out. They are without oil to keep the lamps burning. They turn in desperation to the other five and want them to share the oil they have in reserve for just such a contingency. But the five who had come prepared for a long wait know that if they share their supply, all the lamps will be extinguished before they arrive at the house of the bridegroom. That would certainly dampen the atmosphere of celebration. So while they may regret it, they feel compelled to refuse the request.

The five who did not bring a reserve scurry about to find more oil. Since it is night the shops are closed. By the time they succeed in finding a new supply and return, the wedding party has already entered the house of the bridegroom and the ceremony is underway. When the five maidens arrive and knock on the door, their entrance would be an intrusion and disrupt the gay proceedings. They are denied entrance with the rather harsh reply that they are unknown to the bridegroom.

The parable ends with the admonition to keep awake and be in constant readiness, for the time of the coming of the kingdom is unknown.

Thesis: Prepare for the crisis of the kingdom which may come unexpectedly.

Theme: Seize the day!

Key Words in the Parable

1. "Ten." (v. 1) Numbers in Israel had more of a qualitative meaning than a quantitative designation. Ten was a number of completeness, such as the ten tribes of Israel, the ten commandments and the prescription that where ten adult Jewish males were present in one place, a synagogue should be organized.

2. "Lamps." (v. 1) In biblical imagery lamps are usually identified with the word of God or the witness of the faithful which illuminates and shows direction for life.

3. "Bridegroom." (v. 1) The bridegroom is symbolic in this parable of Jesus. The advent of the kingdom in some special sense was identified with the coming of Jesus, both in his initial appearance in the flesh and in his expected second coming.

4. "Five...foolish; five wise." (v. 2) The indication of half who were wise and half who were foolish probably suggested the incompleteness of the kingdom's manifestation in history. Even in Judaism, and later in the church, not everyone who professed to be obedient to God was really prepared to do so.

5. "Midnight." (v. 6) Midnight is symbolic of the darkest hour, halfway between sundown (6 p.m.) and sunrise (6 a.m.)

6. "Trimmed Their Lamps." (v. 7) The clay lamps had a cotton wick. As the oil was depleted the wick would burn and become black. It had to be trimmed so that it would only burn the oil. Otherwise the lamp would give a dull yellow flame instead of a bright blue flame.

7. "Lord, Lord." (v. 11) Again the euphemism for the name of God is used. It is reminiscent of the vain use of the name by those who mouthed it but were not ready to submit themselves in obedience to the Lord.

8. "I do not Know You." (v. 12) A typical Aramaic expression. It means that I will not have anything to do with you!

9. "Keep Awake." (v. 13) The admonition to keep awake is given just prior to the arrest and trial of Jesus. The disciples slept in the Garden of Gethsemane and consequently were unprepared for the events that followed. They fled and betrayed Jesus. Matthew no doubt was intentional in placing this parable in close proximity to the Garden of Gethsemane events.

Contemplation

Insights

1. Uncertainty. The parable deals with the uncertainty of an event. Uncertainty is one of the chief causes of temptation. So often we can rise to meet a crisis. It is during the time when nothing seems to be happening that we become lax and succumb to temptation. Our fears of anticipation may also be worse than the consequence of the event itself.

2. Apathy. A great enemy of the church is apathy. Many churches have a lot of so-called dead wood. They are people who are on the membership list but do not attend except possibly on the high holy days of Christmas and Easter, or for such events as weddings, baptisms and funerals. They do not contribute more than token amounts to keep their name on the roll. They do not assume any responsibilities for the program of the church. A continuing challenge is to find some way to shout, "Look! Here is the bridegroom. Come out and meet him."

3. State of Readiness. It is hard to maintain a constant state of readiness. Life calls for a rhythm between activity and rest. All ten maidens slept while they waited. Sleeping is not denigrated. In fact, adequate sleep is necessary for readiness. Studies show that people who are sleep deprived over an extended period of time are more prone to accidents and illness, are less efficient in their work and are more irritable. Sleep can, however, be used as an escape from responsibility. Sleep can be interrupted or postponed on occasion for special demands without ill effects.

4. The Unexpected. History is full of surprises. We may see cause and effect in retrospect. It is hard to see the effects of many things in prospect, especially in complex relationships where many factors affect the outcome. One of the most indeterminate factors is the freedom of human responses. The consequences of Jesus' death and resurrection are easier to see with hindsight. How and when the kingdom may break into history in powerful ways in the future cannot be fully anticipated. Therefore it is important to watch and be prepared. The signs of the kingdom's coming into our personal lives or into larger social movements cannot always be perceived in advance to those who are attentive and receptive to them.

5. No Borrowed Oil. The five unprepared maidens wanted the other five to give them some of their oil. They could not do so without running short themselves. One must be careful in pushing details of a parable too hard to fit some notion. If we assume that the oil for the lamps in the parable is symbolic of our works which are the light which shows God's glory, as suggested in Matthew 5:15-16, then the oil for our lamps is our works. The doctrine of supererogation contends that Jesus and certain other persons have earned more merit than they need for salvation. Since salvation is not a matter of merit, but of grace, we do not need to appropriate another's merit. Indeed, we need not and we cannot borrow from another to light our lamps. It is a responsibility we have to be prepared to accept for ourselves.

6. Recognized by the Bridegroom. The foolish maidens who were tardy in arriving at the wedding were not recognized. If we accept the assumption that it is our works that provide the fuel for the light of our lamps, then that light cannot wait until the last moment to be recognized. A time comes when it is too late. If we are citizens of the kingdom, then our character should manifest it. The beatitude says that it is the peacemaker who is a child of God, that is, shares the divine characteristic that demonstrates origin. Character is not acquired instantly. It is the result of a process of actions that lead to recognition of our true parentage.

Homily Hints

1. Oil for My Lamp. (v. 4) We can use a variety of resources to keep our lamp lit.
    A. Prayer and Meditation
    B. Steeping Ourselves in Scripture
    C. Regular Worship
    D. Serving Other's Needs

2. The Bridegroom Comes. (v. 6) Christ comes in many ways to awaken us and invites us to join the wedding banquet.
    A. Through the Examples of Others
    B. Through Events Around Us
    C. Through Personal Failure

3. Trim Your Lamps. (v. 7) People need to rid their lives of the debris that keeps the light from burning true and bright.
    A. Habits of Commission
    B. Habits of Omission
    C. The Burden of Past Guilt

4. Knowing the Day and Hour. (v. 13) Some people are always trying to develop a timetable for the future. They make elaborate schemes purporting to know exactly how and when God will deal with history and its outcome. They do a great deal of mischief by raising false hopes which leads at times to bizarre behavior. We should not fall prey to such false expectations. We do so by being aware of steps to take in response to such schemes.

A. Do not Second Guess God

B. Do not Put God in a Straitjacket

C. Prepare for Any Eventuality

5. The Time is Now. (v. 13) Persons never know with certainty when the time of accountability will come. It may tarry until midnight. It may arrive sooner than we think. It may come as a surprise. Therefore, be alert and ready at all times.

A. Be Awake!

B. Be Watchful!

C. Be at God's Work!

Contact

Points of Contact

1. Reading the Future. People try many ways to read the future. Horoscopes in the daily papers attest to this desire to know how things will happen to us. Tarot cards, fortune cookies, Ouija boards and fortune tellers are some of the means people consult to try to determine their futures. All of these represent a lack of trust that God has the future in hand. For those who are in God's care, the future is not something to fear, but something to enter with confidence. People need to be reassured of this truth.

2. Life as Celebration. People look forward to events which give cause to celebrate — weddings, Christmas, Thanksgiving, Easter, birthdays, anniversaries. People who have had near-death experiences find their life priorities radically altered. Many find the new lease on life a reason to celebrate each new day as an opportunity that might have been lost. Jesus presented life in the kingdom as a royal banquet or as a wedding feast. Christians should not wait for the end of time — either personally or as the Second Coming — to celebrate life. Each day should start with a pause to celebrate the opportunities it brings to live in the kingdom.

3. Lost Opportunity. Fiction writers of short stories, novels, movies and TV programs often dwell on lost opportunities. Because of the development of the plot, the reader or viewer knows before the actors do the tragedy of missing a chance for something that could lead to fulfillment of a desire. In life it is too often only after the event that we know we missed an opportunity — a word not spoken that could have changed a relationship, a bad choice at a critical moment, a wrong direction taken at a juncture in life. Life confronts us with choices and opportunities. None is more important than the choices that affect our eternal destiny. People need to think seriously about how they are prepared for the ultimate choice about the meaning of their lives.

4. Wisdom and Intelligence. Wisdom is not directly correlated with intelligence. Very smart people may not make any better choices in life than those who have lesser intelligence. A person with only marginal intelligence can show love to others and engage in a life of service. The response to the grace of forgiveness and empowerment to live in love, peace, joy, compassion, generosity and other such values can be received by anyone. The wisdom to be prepared to act according to the spirit of Christ is more to be valued than great feats of intelligence without these characteristics.

Points to Ponder

1. Absent Lord. This parable along with others in the series has an absent lord. The bridegroom has not yet appeared. People become atheists because they have no experience which they identify as an experience of the presence of God or as an encounter with Christ in their lives. The problem is to find ways to help them recognize the reality of God. Sometimes it may be an intellectual problem, such as a world view that does not allow for the existence of spiritual realities. It may also be a false conception of who God or Christ must be. It may also result from a poor, distorted or inadequate modeling by those who claim to know God in Christ Jesus. It may also be some ethical or moral barrier in their own lives which will not let God into their lives.

177

2. Awake or Asleep. The parable seems to have an internal inconsistency. All ten maidens are asleep when the shout arises that the bridegroom is coming. It makes no difference whether it is the wise or the foolish maidens. Then in the final verse of the pericope we find the admonition to be awake, as though the point of the parable is not lack of preparedness but being asleep when the Lord comes. Some commentators have suggested that this concluding verse is not part of the original parable, but was appended by Matthew or the early church. How do you harmonize the two? Or do you need to press every detail of a parable for consistency?

3. Maidens and Virgins. In the New Testament it is sometimes a question of how you translate the term which is either maiden or virgin. At the time, the two were considered identical. An unmarried young woman was automatically assumed to be a virgin. In the American culture today, many young people are active sexually at a very young age. It cannot be assumed just on age that a young man or woman is a virgin. Indeed, a growing problem is children having children when they are not mature enough to care for them. They have no stable support unless their parents or other adults provide the support. How should the church address both the problem of early, extra-marital sexual activity and the consequences in infants without the family support needed for them?

Illustrative Materials

1. The End Times. How do you act in anticipation of the end of the world and history as we know it? In the light of the long delay in that end coming, one should prepare as though history will continue for another 2000 years before the eschaton, but should live as though it could happen today.

2. Scout Motto. The scout motto is a good one for Christians also: "Be Prepared."

3. A State of Readiness. During the Cold War the U.S. and the USSR lived in a constant state of readiness for the possibility of a nuclear war. The U.S. Strategic Air Command had planes circling in the air 24 hours a day, 365 days a year to be prepared to respond to a nuclear attack.

4. The Attraction of a Bride. A couple had a two-year-old girl. They were taking her to a botanical garden. On the way they passed a cathedral where a wedding party was evident since the groom and his attendants were standing around in the parking lot. The child was taken inside and saw the bride before the ceremony began. She had no further interest in the botanical garden. She kept wanting to go see the bride again. On the return the doors to the cathedral were open. She was taken where she could see the wedding in progress. Just then the priest began praying and it came over the speakers very loudly. She was somewhat frightened and so they left. She still wanted to see the bride. As they went farther, they walked by the Hilton Hotel. A limousine pulled up with a wedding couple in it. They sat at the entrance without getting out for a while. The young girl was taken over to the limo. The couple opened the window and talked to her briefly. That was a highlight for the two-year-old. She talked about it for a long time afterward.

5. Surprises in History. Malthus developed a theory that the population growth would outstrip the growth of food, resulting in mass death and chaos. Even India and China which were earlier subject to periodic famines have stabilized food production for a much larger population than Malthus would have thought possible.

In the '60s the Club of Rome made some very pessimistic projections about the depletion of oil reserves by the year 2000. Approaching the year 2000 the known oil reserves now are greater than when they made the predictions.

For years many people were expecting that South Africa would

179

only change the apartheid system as the result of a long and bloody civil war. They did not expect it to happen until at least the twenty-first century. The surprise is that the transition took place through a process of political negotiation and a relatively peaceful election.

13. Use It Or Lose It

Matthew 25:14-30

"For it is as if a man, going on a journey, summoned his slaves and entrusted his property to them; [15]to one he gave five talents, to another two, to another one, to each according to his ability. Then he went away. [16]The one who had received the five talents went off at once and traded with them, and made five more talents. [17]In the same way, the one who had the two talents made two more talents. [18]But the one who had received the one talent went off and dug a hole in the ground and hid his master's money. [19]After a long time the master of those slaves came and settled accounts with them. [20]Then the one who had received the five talents came forward, bringing five more talents, saying, 'Master, you handed over to me five talents; see, I have made five more talents.' [21]His master said to him, 'Well done, good and trustworthy slave; you have been trustworthy in a few things, I will put you in charge of many things; enter into the joy of your master.' [22]And the one with the two talents also came forward, saying, 'Master, you handed over to me two talents; see, I have made two more talents.' [23]His master said to him, 'Well done, good and trustworthy slave; you have been trustworthy in a few things, I will put you in charge of many things; enter into the joy of your master.' [24]Then the one who had received the one talent also came forward, saying, 'Master, I knew that you were a harsh man, reaping where you did not sow, and gathering where you did not scatter seed; [25]so I was afraid, and I went and

181

hid your talent in the ground. Here you have what is yours.' ²⁶But his master replied, 'You wicked and lazy slave! You knew, did you, that I reap where I did not sow and gather where I did not scatter? ²⁷Then you ought to have invested my money with the bankers, and on my return I would have received what was my own with interest. ²⁸So take the talent from him, and give it to the one with the ten talents. ²⁹For to all those who have, more will be given, and they will have an abundance; but from those who have nothing, even what they have will be taken away. ³⁰As for this worthless slave, throw him into the outer darkness, where there will be weeping and gnashing of teeth.'"

The parable has given us a new meaning for talents. At the time of the parable it was a unit of measure for silver or gold. Now we have talent shows, talent searches, talent contests. The beauty pageants that came under attack from feminists for being sexist with their emphasis on bathing suit competitions have tried to shift to the talent of the women. Scholarships are offered as prizes so that talented competitors may continue to develop their talents.

Some people still put the emphasis on the monetary nature of the talent which was given to each of the slaves. They find the parable an admonition for stewardship. They stress the importance of investment of money to produce a good return.

A college president was once ruminating on the nature of government and foundation grants. His observation was that the biblical statement that to whom much has been given more will be given was accurate. Some of the neediest colleges that did not have a previous track record of receiving grants had difficulty getting any. Wealthy colleges with large endowments from previous grants seem to have an easy time raising even more money through such grants.

The question arises, of course, as to whether these applications of the parable are what Jesus intended when he told it.

Context

Context of the Scripture

Matthew 25. The parable of the wise and foolish maidens immediately precedes the parable of the faithful and unfaithful slave. In both parables the emphasis is on what should be done while waiting for an absent lord.

The parable of the wise and foolish maidens stresses the importance of preparedness. Having sufficient oil for the lamps stresses the inward nature of the preparation. The parable of the Talents stresses the active, outward use of that which was received from the owner of the property.

Both end with those who were faithful in waiting for the coming of the Lord being rewarded by entering into joy with him.

Matthew 25:14-30 and Luke 19:11-27. The parable of the Talents in Matthew has many similarities to the parable of the Pounds in Luke. They are both set in the latter stages of Jesus' ministry. Luke places it in Jericho as Jesus was headed for the last week in Jerusalem. Matthew has his parable in Jerusalem two days before the Passover.

Both parables address a high expectation that Jesus is about to inaugurate the coming of his kingdom in some significant way. The parables are told to meet that expectation, but at the same time to lessen the expectation of the immediacy of the fullness of the kingdom. The early church no doubt understood the parables as messages telling Jesus' followers what they should be doing in his absence following his death and resurrection.

Some marked differences between the accounts in Matthew and Luke indicate two separate streams of tradition. Matthew says simply that a man was taking a long journey; Luke says it was a nobleman going to receive royal power for himself. In Luke a note is inserted that the nobleman was hated by the citizens and they objected to his rule. Matthew has no such suggestion.

In Matthew the three slaves received differing amounts: five, two and one talent. In Luke each received the same amount.

183

In Matthew the two faithful slaves doubled the amount received. In Luke as in Matthew only three slaves reported on the return of the nobleman but the first doubled the amount while the second only realized 50% return on the ten pounds. In Luke the rewards were commensurate with the earnings. They were given authority over ten and five cities. In Matthew the reward was only approval and participation in the joy of the master.

In both instances the one talent or pound was given to the slave who had earned the larger amount from what was entrusted to him. In the Luke account a protest is registered against giving more to the one who already had the most. No such protest is found in Matthew's account.

Context of the Lectionary

The First Lesson. (Judges 4:1-7) The account is of the reign of Deborah as Judge. The Israelites were subject to King Jabin of Canaan who maintained his rule through Sisera as commander of the army. Deborah orders Barak to confront Sisera with assurance of God's support in the endeavor.

The Second Lesson. (1 Thessalonians 5:1-11) Paul admonishes the Thessalonians to be faithful while waiting for the Lord's coming. They are to avoid the dangers of laxity in guarding against idle and evil activities. They are to support each other in faith, love and hope of salvation through Christ.

The Gospel. (Matthew 25:14-30) The parable is given to make the disciples aware of their accountability even when Jesus would no longer be present.

The Psalm. (Psalm 123) This is a psalm sung as pilgrims came up toward the temple at Jerusalem. It is a plea for the Lord to have mercy on those who were faithful despite the scorn and contempt from others.

Psalm 112:10 — Weeping and gnashing of teeth.
Mark 4:25, Luke 8:18 — Those who have, to them more
    is given; those who have not lose everything.
Romans 12:6-8 — Diversity of gifts.
1 Corinthians 12:4-30 — Varieties of gifts.
Philippians 2:7 — Jesus takes on the form of a slave.
2 Timothy 4:8 — Crown of righteousness is the reward.
Hebrews 12:2 — Jesus at the right hand of God.
Revelation 3:21 — Place on the throne given as reward to
    those who conquer.

Content

Content of the Parable

The content of the parable is probably interpreted differently depending upon when and by whom it was heard.

1. By the Disciples from Jesus. When the disciples heard it, they may have wondered at the story of a man who was going to a far country. They may have thought that they were the slaves who had received the five talents and were faithful in using them. After all, they were the inner circle of Jesus' followers. They may have thought that the other followers who were not as close to Jesus were the two talent people. In the context of the opposition from the scribes and Pharisees, they may have identified them as the one talent slave who was reprimanded. Jesus no doubt intended the parable to be a warning and counsel to the disciples in preparation for his impending death.

2. By the Early Church. When Matthew wrote his gospel the death of Jesus was already about 50 years in the past, more than a typical generation. It was a long time. The church was experiencing persecution and other difficulties. Expectations were high that Jesus would return and establish his kingdom in its fullness.

185

The parable would be a message to continue in faithfulness and activity in anticipation of the reward they would receive at his coming.

3. By the Contemporary Church. Today the delay of Christ's return to bring the kingdom to fulfillment is even longer than for the early church. Many faithful servants would not receive reward for their faithful service if they waited for a second coming. Nevertheless, those who have served Christ and used well the gifts bestowed on them by the Holy Spirit have known the joy of realizing the kingdom in their lives and in the extension of his kingdom on earth. The parable is a message calling for continuing faithfulness in using gifts received from the master.

Precis of the Parable

The kingdom of God is like a man of some wealth who has to take an extended business trip. He calls together three of his trusted workers. He leaves them with the responsibility for managing his business while he is gone.

To the most capable of the three he gives $5000 as working capital. To the next he gives $2000. To the third he gives $1000. As soon as he departs the first two immediately put his capital to work. The third is fearful of his boss. He knows he is a shrewd, hard-nosed entrepreneur. He is fearful that he will lose the $1000 by bad investment. He does not even trust the banks. So he finds a safe place and hides the money so he will be sure to have it when the boss returns.

Eventually the businessman completes his travels and returns. He calls together his three subordinates and asks them to give an accounting. The first two report that they have doubled the original capital. He commends each of them and assures them of tenure in partnership with him. The third comes forward in a fawning manner. He relates how he knows the success of the boss so he played it safe. He hid the money to be sure he would not lose it.

The man is unhappy with the third worker. He scolds him by saying that he should at least have put it in a saving account so it would earn interest. He orders the $1000 transferred to the account of the worker who now had $10,000. He comments that those who do well with what they are entrusted will be given greater responsibility. Those who do not even act responsibly with the little they have will have that taken from them.

The businessman proceeds to fire the third man who goes out to join the multitude of homeless and unemployed.

Thesis: If you don't use your abilities, you lose them.

Theme: It is not how much you have in the kingdom, it is how well you use what you have.

Key Words in the Parable

1. "It." (v. 14) The antecedent to the pronoun goes back to v. 1 of the chapter, referring to the kingdom of heaven.

2. "A Man, Going on a Journey." (v. 14) This is an allusion to the absence of Jesus after his death and resurrection.

3. "Slaves." (v. 14) An allegorical reference to the followers of Jesus who were admonished to be slaves and to find greatness by being a slave to one another.

4. "His Property." (v. 14) The implication is that the Lord as Creator owns the earth and everything in it. We receive the gifts of the earth only in stewardship.

5. "Talent." (v. 15) A talent which was first a unit of measure of silver or gold became the highest denomination of currency. It had the value of 60 times a denarius, thus it was worth about two months' wages.

6. "At Once." (v. 16) The emphasis is on the immediacy of the response of the two faithful slaves. They were like the disciples who dropped their nets and followed Jesus. They were not

187

like the inquirers who hesitated and made excuses when invited to become followers.

7. "Hole in the Ground." (v. 18) Burying treasure was a common way of securing precious items. That was especially true in times of disorder and war. The Dead Sea Scrolls were hidden in that fashion during a time of Roman destruction of Israel and not found until 1948 and later.

8. "Joy." (v. 21) The joy is probably a reference to the heavenly banquet which was a frequent image used for the kingdom of heaven. The first two used their talents without expectation of reward other than the approval of the Lord.

9. "I was Afraid." (v. 25) The fear of the third slave is the key to his failure of character. By not taking any risks he also misses the opportunities for gain.

10. "Outer Darkness." (v. 30) Throwing out the slave to outer darkness is the act of the divine judge, not the man who had gone on a journey. Not to be in the presence of the Lord who is light ultimately leaves the excluded person in darkness.

Contemplation

Insights

1. Personal Freedom. The Master provides us with the resources to use for divine purposes. We are left with the freedom to use them or abuse them. If we know the Master's will and are about his business, we will prosper in our use of the resources. If we neglect or abuse the resources given, we will be held accountable. Rewards are given in proportion to our faithfulness in using well the resources given.

2. Quality vs. Quantity. The parable suggests that it is not the size or quantity of the talents given or the return gained in their use that is the significant factor in the kingdom. It is rather the degree to which we use well that which is given to us. Indeed, the person who has received much has the greater responsibility for using the gifts effectively. In the kingdom it is not the person who has the most wealth or the greatest ability who is considered the greatest. The judgment rendered is according to the proper use of wealth, ability or any other gifts with which a person is endowed. The quality of service is more important than the quantity entrusted to us.

3. The Master's Goods. The parable uses money to make a point about the nature of expectations and rewards. It is not a misuse of the parable to shift the meaning of talents from gold and silver to abilities. The Master's goods extend to the material resources for living. Jesus was never concerned with the spirit alone. He fed the hungry. He turned water to wine at a wedding. He healed the sick. He also gave his disciples spiritual goods. He taught and provided examples for prayer and meditation. He called them to faith and love. He offered forgiveness for sins. These goods are also from the Master and they are given for use in furthering the kingdom.

4. The Adequacy of the Goods. The slaves in the parable were given differing amounts. They received five, two and one talent. The Master knew their abilities and gave them responsibility accordingly. We are assured that God never calls us to a task greater than the goods we are given to do them. We need not shrink back from the task for fear that we do not have the support needed to do it if we truly discern God's call to us. It is more urgent to risk the venture than to bury that which God gives and fail to use whatever we have to do God's work.

5. Waiting and Working. Jesus had a rhythm in his teachings. In the parable of the wise and foolish maidens of last week, the maidens spent some time in waiting for the bridegroom to come. The parable did not say that the waiting was wrong. Jesus himself withdrew from his work with the crowds at times to have solitude and to pray. When Martha was too busy at work to spend time with Jesus, he reprimanded her for her busyness. The parable today implies that the third slave was wicked because he did not put his talent to work. Life calls for a rhythm of waiting and working, both in their proper time and proportion.

Homily Hints

1. Entrusted Property. (v. 14) The Lord gives what belongs to him for our use. People need to take an inventory of what they have received and ask how the good master would have his property used.
- A. Material Goods
- B. Gifts of the Spirit
- C. Personal Relationships
- D. A Base in Organizations

2. One, Two and Five Talents. (v. 15) The parable poses the issue of how persons should consider their contribution to the church and the kingdom. Persons have received a diversity of gifts. All are needed for the fullest realization of what the church and the kingdom should be. It is not the size of the talent that is important. It is more crucial that all contribute according to what they have received.
- A. Making the Most of Money
- B. Making the Most of Time
- C. Making the Most of Abilities

3. The Joy of Your Master. (vv. 21-23) The church should be characterized by joy. Its celebrations should make the members and the world aware that Christian living is a celebration of joy and not a somber and heavy burden to carry.
- A. Celebrate the Presence of Christ
- B. Celebrate the Approval of Christ
- C. Celebrate the Participation in Christ
- D. Celebrate the Anticipation of Christ

4. I Was Afraid. (v. 25) Too often people consult their fears and condition their actions on them. They should look at what led the third slave to hide the talent instead of investing it to prosper the master's kingdom. Some are afraid of failure. Others are afraid of success because it might bring more responsibilities which they do not want to accept.

    A. He did not Understand His Master

    B. He Lacked a Spirit of Adventure

    C. He Lacked a Readiness for Growth

5. Living with Abundance. (v. 29) The five talent slave enjoyed the abundance conferred on him by the master. How do we accept the abundance and live with it?

    A. Live with Humility

    B. Live Cheerfully

    C. Live Responsibly

    D. Live Christ-like

6. Thrown into Outer Darkness. (v. 30) Christians should not be sentimental about what it means to fail to live as a follower of Christ. The consequences are harsh and real. The outer darkness is a symbol of how life is experienced without the abundant gifts of faith, hope and love.

    A. The Occasion for Fear. The fear of being left on our own.

    B. The Sense of Failure. The recognition that one has missed the ultimate meaning of life.

    C. The Feeling of Futility. Life is but sound and fury without hope and what one does eventually passes away if it is not sustained by the Lord of the universe.

    D. The Antidote to Fear. It is to have confidence that trust and response to the master is a source of approval and joy.

Contact

Points of Contact

    1. The joy which the faithful slaves received comes not

from the immediacy of pleasure. It comes from the deeper sources of life. They had the satisfaction of accomplishing a task and being approved as persons of worth. Pleasure that comes from such things as good food, the thrill of exciting activities and similar sources lasts only briefly. They do not give the same underlying joy that can be found in the midst of toil and difficulty. Jesus had an air of joy about him that attracted people even while he labored and encountered opposition. Persons who have the security of trust in him and awareness of his presence have a serenity despite the troubled world in which they live. This brings a kind of enduring satisfaction that transitory pleasures cannot afford.

2. Life requires growth. When we stop growing we begin dying. Muscles that are not used begin to atrophy. Abilities not used begin to fade. Skills not practiced lose their edge. It can be said that a basic law of life is that you must use what you have or you lose it. The converse of the law is that those who use what they have gain more and more.

3. Salvation may be given in an experience of a moment. But to retain it, it must result in continuing growth. While Paul had a momentous experience on the Damascus Road, he had to spend a lengthy period in Arabia to work out the full meaning of the encounter with Christ. He also consulted with the Apostles in Jerusalem before he was ready to perform his great missionary works. People have to invest their talents in working out their salvation once it has been given to them. Those who are born again in Christ need to grow up to the fullness of maturity in him.

Points to Ponder

1. A challenge to consider is whether we can double the return on the talents given us. That takes some risk in trying to use them. It also takes time and may seem that we are acting on our own without guidance and support. How do you persevere in such circumstances?

2. What do you do when you experience the absence of Christ in your life? Almost everyone has periods of spiritual dryness. It feels as though they are no longer in touch with God. Is it a time of testing of faith and trust? What kinds of patience and waiting do we have to exercise in the expectation that the absent Lord will return to us? What kinds of disciplines can we follow which will help us recover the awareness of his presence in our life again?

3. All men (persons) are created equal according to the Declaration of Independence. Yet it seems obvious that not everyone is equally endowed. The parable says that the slaves had differing amounts with which to work for the master. Is equality to be thought of in terms of opportunity to fulfill their possibilities? Or is it in approval for how they perform with what they have? Or is it in ultimate worth before God as persons of value?

4. The judgment pronounced on the slave who tried to protect the talent was severe. He was called wicked and lazy. We usually do not associate wickedness with lack of action. We tend to think of it as some dastardly actions which do injury and harm to others. We do not usually assume that it applies to what we fail to do in using the gifts granted to us. The consequence of being thrown into outer darkness seems contrary to the general image of a heavenly Father who is merciful, compassionate and forgiving. How do we reconcile this image of the Lord with John's statement that God is love?

5. How do you cope with the feelings of members of the church who think that what they have to contribute is of little worth? They may compare themselves with the people who can perform before the whole congregation: the eloquent preacher, the competent choir director, the beautiful voice of the soloist, the charismatic teacher. Some members may resent those who are elected or appointed to positions of prominence. How does the church recognize and approve the services of the one talent person who makes good use of what he or she has?

1. Use It or Lose It. A long distance jogger has to start slowly and build up to the capacity to run several miles. The experts advise that one needs to run three to five days a week, with days in between to recover. If one ceases running, however, in three days one is already losing muscle tone. In three weeks one needs to start over to rebuild stamina.

———————————

Recent research with persons in retirement homes demonstrates that exercise restores bone structure. With weight lifting, even persons in the late eighties or early nineties have shown improvement. Some who were using walkers or were confined to wheelchairs found that they could walk unaided again.

2. Use the Talent You Have. A football star for a college team was having trouble in a course on church history. He was barely doing C work. He came to see the professor about the problem. The professor knew he had some limited ability and preparation. The student had dropped out of high school and obtained a General Equivalency Diploma in the armed forces so he could enter college. The professor pointed out, however, that he was not necessarily expected to be a star in every area. What he should do is the best he could with the abilities he had. Just because he could run faster than anyone else on the football team did not mean he could beat everyone in the classroom. He should be satisfied that he had put forth his best effort and did the best he could. He accepted the counsel and in fact got a low B in the course. Later when he became a professional football player with records for touchdowns scored, he still visited that professor when he returned to campus.

3. Servanthood. A church executive headed a large church agency for years. He was well-known and highly respected throughout his denomination and in larger church circles. Eventually he came to the age where his energies and abilities diminished. Upon his retirement he found satisfaction in assuming the job of janitor in the congregation to which he belonged. He expressed his gratitude for being able to serve the church in that way after years of benefiting from the services of others who did that kind of work.

———————————

A missionary to India came to the age of retirement. To supplement his income he became the custodian of the church in the community where he retired. He kept the building in tip-top shape. In a quiet way he became a presence in the church and community. His service was a role model of modesty, competence and devotion to his work. He gave witness by this ministry. Everyone understood why he had been an effective missionary.

4. Approval for Service. The Director of Christian Education was telling a story about the importance of doing work in the church. At one point she turned to the children and asked, "Now who is doing the most important work in our church?" Immediately one of the younger children piped up so the whole congregation could hear, "The janitor." After a brief pause, everyone burst into laughter and applause. It was an affirmation of what the child said to the delight of the red-faced janitor!

14. Actions Determine Judgment

Matthew 25:31-46

---

*"When the Son of Man comes in his glory, and
all the angels with him, then he will sit on the throne of
his glory. [32]All the nations will be gathered before him,
and he will separate people one from another as a shepherd separates the sheep from the goats, [33]and he will
put the sheep at his right hand and the goats at the left.
[34]Then the king will say to those at his right hand,
'Come, you that are blessed by my Father, inherit the
kingdom prepared for you from the foundation of the
world; [35]for I was hungry and you gave me food, I was
thirsty and you gave me something to drink, I was a
stranger and you welcomed me, [36]I was naked and you
gave me clothing, I was sick and you took care of me, I
was in prison and you visited me.' [37]Then the righteous will answer him, 'Lord, when was it that we saw
you hungry and gave you food, or thirsty and gave you
something to drink? [38]And when was it that we saw
you a stranger and welcomed you, or naked and gave
you clothing? [39]And when was it that we saw you sick
or in prison and visited you?' [40]And the king will answer them, 'Truly I tell you, just as you did it to one of
the least of these who are members of my family, you
did it to me.' [41]Then he will say to those at his left
hand, 'You that are accursed, depart from me into the
eternal fire prepared for the devil and his angels; [42]for
I was hungry and you gave me no food, I was thirsty
and you gave me nothing to drink, [43]I was a stranger
and you did not welcome me, naked and you did not*

give me clothing, sick and in prison and you did not
visit me.' ⁴⁴Then they also will answer, 'Lord, when
was it that we saw you hungry or thirsty or a stranger
or naked or sick or in prison, and did not take care of
you?' ⁴⁵Then he will answer them, 'Truly I tell you,
just as you did not do it to one of the least of these, you
did not do it to me.' ⁴⁶And these will go away into eter-
nal punishment, but the righteous into eternal life."

The parable brings us to the end of the parables in Cycle A
of the lectionary. It is also the end of the last block of teaching
material in the Gospel according to Matthew. It is appropriate that
the parable points to the final judgment, the outcome of all that
Jesus was trying to teach and demonstrate about the meaning of
the kingdom of heaven.

The parable contains some rich contrasts in the imagery it
uses. On the one hand is the image of the king and the hosts of
heaven. It is a picture of a royal court where judgment is being
dispensed. All the peoples of the earth are on trial and sentence is
being pronounced.

On the other hand, the image is from a simple pastoral
scene that could be seen every day in Palestine. The picture is of a
herd of sheep and goats. They are animals quite different in tem-
perament and activity. Even the casual observer could tell them
apart.

The contrasting imagery was striking and would stick in
the memory of those who heard it. It contains for us the same
striking quality. At the same time it communicates some of the
most profound insights into Jesus' view of what religion and life
are all about.

Context

Context of the Church Year

The church year begins with the expectation of the coming
of the Christ child. The year proceeds through the Lenten period in

the preparation for the passion of Jesus. It reaches a climax in the crucifixion which has the supposedly ironic tag of Jesus as the King of the Jews.

The year moves on through the resurrection and ascension events. Then comes Pentecost with the continuation of Jesus' ministry through the founding and establishing of the church. The kingship of Christ is affirmed in the church's confession that Jesus is Lord.

The year comes to an end by portraying the outcome of human history in a final judgment. The parable asserts the kingship and glory of Christ over all the peoples. His kingship is not arbitrary or transient. It is integral to the universe itself. It rests on the very foundation of the world (Matthew 25:34).

Context of Matthew

The birth story of Jesus in Matthew emphasizes the royalty of Jesus. It is stressed again in the triumphal entry into Jerusalem which occurred just shortly before the telling of the parable. In the parable Matthew makes clear the recognition of Christ as King.

In Matthew 25 we have three parables of the kingdom:
> Matthew 25:1-13 — The necessity for being prepared.
> Matthew 25:14-30 — The call to accountability.
> Matthew 25:31-46 — The sentence pronounced.

Context of the Lectionary

The First Lesson. (Ezekiel 34:11-16, 20-24) The passage presents the image of God as the true shepherd. The people are like rambunctious sheep that need to be brought into line. The Lord appoints a David figure to judge the sheep and care for them so that they are not scattered and ravaged.

The Second Lesson. (Ephesians 1:15-23) The passage claims that it is the power of Christ which is at work in the church. It prepares the church for the inheritance of glory among the saints.

It claims that the resurrection is confirmation of the rule of Christ both in this age and the age to come.

Gospel. (Matthew 25:31-46) Christ returns in glory with all the angels. He holds court with all the peoples as defendants. He separates them as a shepherd would separate sheep and goats. The criteria is their service or lack of it for the poor, oppressed, captive and needy as representatives of him. The sheep are gathered into the kingdom. The goats are sent to eternal punishment.

Psalm. (Psalm 100) The psalm is a song of praise as the people enter the temple. They gather as sheep to give God thanks and to acknowledge his steadfast love and faithfulness.

Context of Related Scripture

> 1 Kings 19:22 — The Lord is sitting on his throne with the heavenly host.
> Joel 3:2, 11-12 — Judging of the nations.
> Zechariah 14:2-5 — The Lord battles against all the nations and comes with all the holy ones.
> Matthew 5:3, 5 — The blessed inherit the kingdom.
> Luke 10:30-37 — The good Samaritan approved for showing mercy.
> James 1:27 — Pure religion defined as caring for widows and orphans in distress.
> 1 John 3:17 — A rhetorical question implying that anyone who has the world's goods and does not help brothers and sisters in need does not have God's love.
> Revelation 20:9-10 — A lake of fire and sulphur prepared for Satan and the people who follow him.
> Revelation 21:8 — A lake of fire and sulphur as a place for the various wicked persons.

Content

Content of the Parable

Many moderns will find the judgment of those who neglect to minister to the needs of people harsh. Some of the biblical language used to communicate the severity of consequences when persons neglect to show compassion and practice charity, as this parable does, is very graphic. In an age when democracy is touted as the ideal and arbitrary royal authority is in disrepute, persons may have trouble with the portrayal of God as a king with his retinue in all their splendor.

A god who holds court and dispenses summary judgment would be much more familiar to the people who heard the parable originally. They would readily understand that such actions were the prerogative of the highest authority. The prophets had portrayed God as a judge over Israel and the nations around it.

Nevertheless, the message of Jesus is clear. Actions display the true character of persons. How they behave has consequences in the formation of personality. It is their personality that endures and has permanence. Continued ignoring of the needs of others has a corroding affect that eventually leaves persons alienated and alone. Callousness to the needs of others burns away the spirit and the light within a person.

The consequences are not arbitrary. They are the inevitable outcome of habitual action.

Precis of the Parable

The Son of Man comes at the end of history with his messengers to judge all the peoples of the world. As a shepherd divides the irascible goats from the more tractable sheep, so the people are separated with the favored people being the sheep and those judged out of favor as the goats.

The Lord passes judgment on the people according to their behavior toward the hungry, the thirsty, the alien, the naked, the sick and the prisoner. Those who met the needs of those victims were gathered into the eternal kingdom, to their surprise. They are told that as they acted toward those needy people, it was considered an act toward God.

Those who were judged out of favor ignored the needs of these unfortunate persons. They too were surprised to find that their lack of action sealed their eternal fate.

The parable ends with the sentence of eternal life for the righteous and eternal punishment for those out of favor for their lack of compassionate action.

Thesis: Judgment of life is based on the treatment of the poor and oppressed.

Theme: Charity toward the needy is the basis of righteousness.

Key Words in the Parable

1. "Son of Man." (v. 31) The apocalyptic title used by Jesus to indicate both his humble humanity and the divine power and glory given to him in his eternal being. It was the favorite title found only on the lips of Jesus with reference to himself. It appears in that way on every level of Gospel tradition.

2. "Angels." (v. 31) The term is a transliteration of the Greek word for *messengers*. They are agents of God to make known or to do his will among people.

3. "All the Nations Will be Gathered." (v. 32) The nations are not political units defined by territory as in the modern nation-state. They are the non-Jewish ethnic groups in the world.

4. "Sheep and Goats." (vv. 32-33) The sheep in Palestine were white and the goats were black. It would be easy to separate them by color. They also had differing characteristics. Goats are more active, combative, ill-scented. Sheep are more passive, submissive and patient. Sheep were considered more valuable than goats.

5. "Right hand." (v. 34) In a population that is predominantly right-handed, those seated at the right hand of the king exercised the same power as the king. The word *sinister* in English comes from the Latin word for left-handed: *sinistra*. Persons who were left-handed did not act in the accustomed and expected manner. Therefore they were suspect.

6. "I was hungry ..." (v. 35) The I is the emphatic form of the pronoun. It refers to who is Jesus.

7. "The Eternal Fire." (v. 41) The symbol for the place of punishment was Gahenna. It was a valley outside of Jerusalem where the trash and garbage were dumped. It burned constantly with much smoke and an acrid smell. The eternal fire was the place for the trash and garbage of history.

8. "The Devil and His Angels." (v. 41) The Devil and his angels are the adversaries of God. According to earlier writings they had been associates of God who rebelled against his authority and were cast out of heaven to a place of condemnation.

Contemplation

1. The Humanity of Jesus. Various titles are given in the parable: The Son of Man (v. 31), Shepherd (vv. 32, 34) and Lord (v. 37). In these titles you have both the humanity of Jesus and his divinity. To the Greeks it was scandalous to say that the divine could be found in a human being. Docetism posited numerous subordinate beings separating divinity from the corruption of the material world, which included human beings. To them Jesus only appeared to be a human being. Divinity in their understanding could not have an evil, corruptible body. To the Hebrews it was blasphemous to say that a human being could be divine. Jesus demonstrated that humanity and divinity were compatible.

To say that Jesus had two natures, human and divine, may present a mathematical or logical problem as to how the two could be one in Christ. Reality does not present such a problem. Jesus testified to the possibility that human nature at its highest and best can be godlike.

2. The Ethics of Jesus. The ethics of Jesus started with his humanity. He knew the human condition and addressed the full range of human needs. He did not separate physical needs from spiritual needs. He showed compassion for those who were hungry, thirsty, naked or sick.

He ended his ethics with his divinity. He addressed the spiritual condition of sin, addiction and bondage. He looked at persons and saw their possibilities for fulfillment as God intended them in creation. He acted to bring people to their highest potential regardless of race, ethnicity, nationality, gender, social status or economic class.

3. The Love of Jesus. Jesus' ethic was grounded in his humanity. It was powered by a love that was divine. He was not simply a humanist who thought people could be saved by their own efforts. To minister to the needs of people who did not always act nicely or behave well he had to tap the resources of the Father. His love enabled him to love even those who opposed him and sought him ill, even his death. His message of judgment was not vindictive or vengeful. It was intended as a warning to bring people to an awareness of the end to which they were tending. Then they could repent and, with God's help through the Holy Spirit, realize their highest destiny.

4. Hidden Opportunity. The same humanity found in Jesus is found even in what appears from the human view to be the least of persons. Jesus saw in the human need both an opportunity to help to fulfill their humanity and at the same time afford the actors to demonstrate by their ministry of Christian love their own divinity. Every person in need whom we are able to help represents a hidden opportunity for us to be a channel of God's loving redemption and thereby to unleash in ourselves the character of the divine.

5. The Foundation of the World. Physically, the scientist may look at the foundation of the world in some big bang theory, in some characteristic of matter that can expand and fill the universe. Spiritually, we look to a God of love, mercy and compassion at the foundation of the world. The personal foundation of the world is in the source of life in all of its richness and diversity. It reaches its apex in beings who are conscious, free and have a capacity to support, encourage and sustain life at its personal fullest.

6. I am My Brother and Sister. Cain asked the question, "Am I my brother's keeper?" Jesus in this parable goes beyond that query. He says, "I am my brother and sister." A chief characteristic of personal beings is their capacity to jump out of their existential skin and identify with another being. To the degree that we can experience the suffering and joy of other persons, we ourselves exercise our personhood. The more we identify ourselves with our brothers and sisters, the more completely we are persons. We move beyond treating others as mere objects to be used by us to meet our need and identify them as ends in themselves. To enable them to come to their greatest possibilities we say that I am my brother and sister.

Homily Hints

1. Who is on God's Side? (v. 33) The sheep were put at God's right hand. They are to use the power of God as if it were their own because they were acting according to the nature of God. The question posed is: Who is on God's side acting for his purposes and who is on the devil's side and acting for him?

A. The Character of the Lord — Love.
B. The Character of the Devil — Self-Centered.
C. Our Character — Love which is Other-centered.

2. The Hidden Test. (vv. 40, 45) The person in need whom I meet and can help is God's test of my fullest humanity. Only our habitual, unselfconcious response to every human need passes the test.

A. The Test in the Poor
B. The Test in the Sick
C. The Test in the Prisoner
D. Meeting the Test

3. Recognizing Jesus. (vv. 35-46) If Jesus would return today as he came when in the flesh, would we recognize him as the disciples did? Or would we be part of the scribes and Pharisees who rejected him?

    A. Recognizing Him by His Humanity
        1. By His Compassion
        2. By His Love
        3. By His Service
    B. Recognizing Him by His Divinity
        1. By His Glory
        2. By His Implicit Judgment
        3. By His Spiritual Power
    C. Recognizing Him in Our Neighbor

4. Surprised Saints and Surprised Sinners. (vv. 37, 44) Both those who found favor with the king and those who were in disfavor were unaware that what they were doing or lacked doing was God's work.

    A. Surprised Saints
    B. Surprised Sinners
    C. No Surprises for Us

5. The Trash Heap of History. (v. 41) Gahenna was the trash and garbage dump of Jerusalem. With its smoke, smell and flames, it became the vivid image for hell. Jesus proposed in the parable that those who ignore the need of fellow human beings are destined for the trash heap of history.

    A. Who Does the World Honor?
    B. Who Does Christ Honor?
    C. Do We Honor Who Christ Honors?
    D. Who Ends on the Trash Heap Without Honor?

Contact

1. The human tendency is to judge people's worth. It is easy to consider the poor, the weak, the persons with disabilities, the persons of different racial or ethnic characteristics from our own as less worthy. We can know how they feel when we experience a similar demeaning in our own relations with others.

The way to overcome our own feelings of alienation and hurt from such actions is to change our attitudes toward others who are rejected and oppressed. We find our own worth by seeing the worth of even the least of the others in the typical human response. When we see the opportunity to help the others become fully human, we respect and give worth to our own humanity.

2. Each of us has a dark side and a light side. We have a duality in our own natures. We know at our deepest being that we do not want condemnation for that part of us that is dark. Generally we try to hide it and to present ourselves from our light side so that we will be accepted. We want help to be released from the dark impulses that we feel.

It is not condemnation but salvation that we really desire. From that personal awareness we can understand that it is also the condition of others. Out of that awareness we act to offer help to others rather than condemnation and rejection. When we do, the power of the Holy Spirit within us helps the light side to overcome the dark side in us and the other.

3. The Word became flesh according to John 1. We generally refer to that as the incarnation, as it comes from the Latin word *carnes* which is the English word flesh. The doctrine of incarnation is the affirmation that the divine can be expressed in the human. The two are compatible. Salvation is the reverse process of the incarnation. We call the process sanctification, becoming holy. As in Jesus Christ, the divine became human, so in salvation and sanctification the human becomes as fully divine as our humanity allows. To the degree that we become like Jesus in our spiritual nature, we engage in the reverse reaction of the Word becoming flesh.

4. The world's need offers us abundant opportunities to engage in Christ-like activity. We do not have to go searching for ways to serve Christ. They come searching for us. As we respond to the smallest of needs that meet us face to face, we become increasingly aware of the larger needs of the world around us and beyond our immediate environment. They provide us with opportunities to grow in Christ-likeness.

As we act to meet the needs that we can, the response will become habitual and second nature to us. If we make a regular practice of letting human need guide our life's purposes and goals, we will be surprised that anyone would think that it is something special or worthy of note. Then we know that Christ's spirit indwells our spirit.

Points to Ponder

1. Shepherd or Judge. In the parable the sheep and goats are separated by the shepherd. The shepherd becomes a judge who relegates the goats to eternal punishment that seems to be rather harsh and a shift from the shepherd who cares for his flock. He becomes a judge who condemns and sentences to punishment. One New Testament scholar has proposed that in his earthly ministry Jesus came as the savior shepherd. At the end of history he will appear as the kingly judge. How do you harmonize the saving action and the judging face of Christ?

2. The Criteria for Judgment. The sheep and the goats are divided on the basis of their actions. It seems that the ultimate criteria for salvation to eternal life or condemnation to eternal punishment is our deeds. Is this a works righteousness? Is Jesus only speaking in the parable about the nations, that is, the non-Jews or those not his disciples who are ignorant of the law and the gospel? Is this the criteria for those who only act according to the light they have received without having the benefit of the direct knowledge of Jesus Christ and the scriptures?

3. Individual Action and Policy Decisions. The parable

addresses only responses to individual persons. It does not address large scale programs, organized institutions or policy decisions which affect the hungry, the thirsty, the naked, the sick and the prisoner. Is it better from a religious point of view to minister to the persons we meet and know, or would it be better to establish institutions and influence policy decisions which would eliminate the cause of the problems or take care of them in a more systematic way? What role does influencing government programs and policies which operate on a societal scale have in serving the least of the ones with whom Jesus identified himself? The church has often established institutions to minister to the needs of people in an organized and systematic way. Later the state has seen these models as legitimate activities for it to meet the needs of its citizens. Is it a proper function of the church to pioneer with such models and let the state assume responsibility for doing work in this way on a larger scale? Examples would include schools, orphanages, mental institutions and hospitals.

Illustrative Material

1. Overwhelmed by Need. In the '60s Norman Cousins visited India. He was overwhelmed by the massive need he observed on this subcontinent. He puzzled over the question of whether he could in any way do something to meet the needs which he saw. He concluded that what he could do was to meet the need of the individual who addressed him personally. He felt a responsibility to meet the need that he could select because it confronted him personally even if he could not correct the situation of every need in the world.

2. A Scriptural Machine Gun. Jesus confronted the scribes and Pharisees who knew and observed the law. They did not, however, meet the needs of the poor and oppressed. A minister in characterizing a certain person described her as a scriptural machine gun. She could mow down persons who disagreed with her by quoting scripture and condemning them. However, she lacked the grace and compassion to identify with the need of the persons.

3. Mad with Love for God and Men.

The following is from *Kagawa* by William Axling.

> *Kagawa took his friends by sudden surprise when at the age of twenty-one he took a straight header into the depths of the Shinkawa slums. Here ten thousand people were sardined into houses six feet square, more like prison cells than homes.... Their income averaged from twenty-five to fifty cents a day when work was available, but much time was spent in enforced idleness. The district swarmed with under-nourished children, covered from head to foot with scrofula and various kinds of skin diseases.... Day and night, disease of every description did its deadly work all over this area....*
>
> *When once the young Kagawa found himself in the slums, the desire to give his life for the underprivileged, which had been taking root in his soul for many a month, burst into a full-blown purpose. Persecuted and threatened, he stood unmoved. He feared neither man, vermin, filth, nor disease. The itch, the pest, tuberculosis, syphilis—he lived, slept, and moved among them. He had made up his mind that his lifespan was to be short at the best, and faced it all without anxiety or fear.... He gloried in the belief that Christianity is not a religion of sensible men, but of men gone mad with love for God and man.[1]*

4. Victim Offender Reconciliation Program.

The Victim Offender Reconciliation Program (VORP) has had some remarkable success in bringing victims and those who perpetrated crimes against them together. When the criminal confronts his or her victims in the presence of a trained, third party mediator some interesting things happen. The criminals often come to recognize the pain and harm they have done to the victims, which they had not thought about before. They come to understand and relate to them as persons. In many cases the criminal has repented, made some restitution and been reconciled with the victims. For the victims the encounter has also had a therapeutic effect. It removes the fear, the hatred and the continuing anguish that makes them permanent victims. Both parties then receive some healing in the process.

---

[1]William Axling, *Kagawa*, (New York: Harper and Brothers) in Kirby Page, *Living Abundantly*, (New York: Farrar and Rinehart, 1994), p. 382f.